The Lion's Roar

Asian Thought and Culture

Charles Wei-hsun Fu
General Editor

Vol. VI

PETER LANG
New York · San Francisco · Bern
Frankfurt am Main · Paris · London

Venerable Master Hsing Yun

The Lion's Roar

Actualizing Buddhism in Daily Life and Building the Pure Land in Our Midst

PETER LANG
New York · San Francisco · Bern
Frankfurt am Main · Paris · London

Library of Congress Cataloging-in-Publication Data

Hsing-yun-ta shih.
    The lion's roar : actualizing Buddhism in daily life and
building the pure land in our midst : ch'an talks / Hsing
Yun: translated by Yung Kai, Chen Xin;

        p. cm. — (Asian thought and culture ; vol. 6)
    Includes bibliographical references and index.
    I. Zen Buddhism.   2. Koan.   I. Fu, Charles Wei-hsun,
1933- II. Title. III. Series.
    BQ9266.H76   1991   294.3'44—dc20   90-25346
    ISBN 0-8204-1544-8   CIP
    ISSN 0893-6870

The paper in this book meets the guidelines for permanence and durability
of the Committee on Production Guidelines for Book Longevity of
the Council on Library Resources.

CONTENTS

PREFACE

At home, if we arrange some elegant and fragrant flowers in a clean, cozy living room, they will exude vitality and vigor. If we hang a traditional Chinese landscape painting on the wall, depicting ridges and peaks veiled in clouds and snow, the white, spacious wall will seem to embrace mountains and rivers. Similarly, if we add some seasoning to an appetizing dish, it will become more delicious. Ch'an is just like the flowers, the painting, and the seasoning! When life is complemented by the flavor of Ch'an, the meaning of life will be grasped all the more clearly. As one poet states: "The moon outside the window is always the same, but it looks more brilliant when the plum flowers are in bloom."

Living in our bustling, intense, turbulent, and chaotic contemporary society, we need to find something that can set our impetuous minds at ease. Ch'an is undoubtedly such a force; it can free us from anxiety and misgivings, as well as exert a calming effect on our minds and souls. Ch'an reflects wisdom, humor, and compassion. It can prevent the formation of wishful and vexing thoughts. Guided by the ease, humor, profundity, and liberating nature of Ch'an, one will not be bothered by unkind words, awkward behavior, or painful memories of the past. They will simply vanish like mist and smoke.

Ch'an raises life to the level of art. It manifests the perfection of life by revealing the original nature that underlies all phenomena. Ch'an's exquisite teaching is not confined to temples, nor is it to be enjoyed solely by monks and nuns. It belongs to every family and to every human being. Everyone is in need of its wisdom, spontaneity, freedom, and ethics in his or her daily life.

At the request of Buddhists, both in Taiwan and abroad, I have in recent years tried to disclose the profound implications of Ch'an. I also have given lectures on an important work of the Ch'an School—*The Sixth Patriarch's Platform Sutra*—on Taiwanese television. Responses to the program have been enthusiastic, indicating that people from all walks of life yearn for the teachings of Ch'an. Thus, I was invited to write a daily *kung-an* for the *Evening News*. Over a year's time, more than three hundred articles were written. These were collected and published under the title *Master Hsing Yun's Account of Ch'an*. Simultaneously, the articles were reprinted in the *World Journal* (Daily News) and distributed in both the United States and Thailand. It then was suggested that *Master Hsing Yun's Account of Ch'an* be made into a television program so that more people would be able to appreciate the liberating qualities of Ch'an. The program "Master Hsing Yun's Account of Ch'an" made its debut in April, 1986. At present, more than two hundred episodes have been made.

Since the commentaries that comprise this account were written and filmed during breaks in my travels, they are far from perfect. My *Accounts* will continue to be published and filmed; hence, I expect that the unsatisfactory parts will be revised. Fortunately, Ch'an eschews dogmatic scriptures, for its connotations reach beyond the scope of words. I hope the readers will be able to read between the lines and appreciate the subtle yet profound effects and implications of Ch'an that can be incorporated into their own lives.

Recently, I was urged to offer these stories to the English-speaking public through translations in order that more people would have the opportunity to appreciate the wisdom of Ch'an. Although these witty *kung-an*s can be enjoyed without any extensive background in Buddhist philosophy, endnotes and a glossary of key terminology have been appended to the original text to enrich the experience. Thus, this volume serves as a fitting introduction to the wonders of Ch'an. An attempt has been made to keep the introduction of new words within reasonable limits. Certain Chinese and Sanskrit terms have been used for a lack of better English translations. Diacritical marks for some Sanskrit terms have been kept, whereas words that have made their way into standard English dictionaries will appear without the marks.

This volume represents the combined efforts of many individuals working toward the common goal of preparing the text for the English-reading public. I would like to take this opportunity to thank the many people who have been involved in the process. Venerable Yung Kai provided the initial translation of stories one through ninety-nine and also supervised the publication process, while stories one hundred through 195 were first translated by Chen Xin from the University of Hawaii. Professor Charles Wei-hsun Fu of Temple University and Professor Sandra Wawrytko of San Diego State University were very kind and generous in providing suggestions for the style and layout and made coordinations with the publisher. Refinements to several chapters were contributed by students of the Ts'ung Lin Buddhist College at Fo Kuang Shan Temple in the course of a class on English translation during the summer of 1990. Venerable Hui Kai rendered invaluable service in reviewing the overall text and comparing it with the Chinese original. Marina Leung, Kelly Chock, and students of the meditation class at Hsi Lai Temple have contributed tremendously by proofreading the manuscript and providing their invaluable suggestions. I am indebted to each of these individuals for their generous support and cooperation.

Hsing Yun
April, 1991
Los Angeles, California

Is the Wind or the Banner Moving?

After inheriting the robe and bowl,[1] Ch'an Master Hui-nêng hid among a band of hunters for over ten years. When the time was ripe, he started to teach the Dharma.

One day, Hui-nêng arrived at Fa-hsing Temple and saw two monks arguing heatedly in front of a banner. Hui-nêng approached them, listening to their argument. One of the monks said, "If there is no wind, how can the banner move? Therefore, I say it is the wind that is moving."

The other retorted, "If there is no banner, how can you know that the wind is moving? So I say it is the banner that is moving."

Each insisted that his own view was the correct one.

Hui-nêng interrupted them and said, "Please, there is no need to argue. I would like to settle the matter for you. It is neither the wind that is moving, nor is it the banner that is moving. It is your minds that are moving!"

It can be seen from this *kung-an* that a Ch'an master's way of looking at phenomena is not confined to external appearances. Ch'an masters see things through the mind's eye.

Our views differ because of our discriminating minds. When our minds are still, all things are at peace. When our minds move, various distinctions arise. To reach the state in which stillness and non-stillness harmonize, we have to eradicate ourselves of all discriminating thoughts. Only then will the peacefulness and stillness of nirvana be realized.

Not Accepting Responsibility

Late one evening, Ch'an Master Li-tsung stood in front of the monks' dormitory and shouted, "Thief! Thief!"

Everyone was awakened by the uproar. Instantly, a monk came running out of the dormitory. Ch'an Master Li-tsung grabbed hold of him and screamed, "I caught him! I caught the thief!"

The monk protested, "Master, you have caught the wrong person! I am not the thief!"

Li-tsung would not release him and said loudly, "Yes, you are! Why won't you admit it?"

The monk was so afraid that he did not know what to do. Master Li-tsung recited a verse:

> Thirty years around Lake Hsi-tzŭ,
> The two meals increased our strength.
> You came up to the mountain for nothing!
> May I ask, do you understand or not?

There is a Buddhist saying: "To catch a mountain thief is easy, but to catch the thief[2] of the mind is very difficult." In our everyday living, we often use our eyes, ears, nose, tongue, body, and mind to seek the pleasures of color, sound, smell, taste, touch, and thought, respectively. Thus, defilements and suffering arise.

The purpose of practicing the Dharma and taking meals daily for thirty years was to subdue the thief of the mind. If we can understand this and are capable of going to the mountain to practice so that we can catch the thief of our minds, this would indeed be the true Dharma! Master Li-tsung's way of testing the monk was truly a manifestation of the greatness of Ch'an masters.

> Thieves linger day and night,
> Outside the doors of our six roots[3];
> If we go out into the streets for nothing,
> Who will take responsibility when trouble
>   arises?

How can we guard the doors of our six roots day and night so that they do not go astray? This task should not be neglected by a Ch'an practitioner.

Does the Master Look Like a Donkey?

When Ch'an Master Kuang-yung first went to visit Ch'an Master Yang-shan, the latter asked him, "What is the purpose of your visit?"

Kuang-yung answered, "I came to pay my respects to the Master."

Then Yang-shan inquired, "Have you seen the Master?"

Kuang-yung replied, "Yes, I have."

"Does the Master look like a donkey or a horse?"

Kuang-yung answered, "It seems to me that the Master does not look like a Buddha either!"

Yang-shan insisted, "If the Master does not look like a Buddha, then what does he look like?"

Kuang-yung replied, "If he looked like something, then he would be no different from a donkey or a horse."

Surprised, Yang-shan declared, "One should forget the difference between a Buddha and an average person and overcome all passions. Then one's true nature will shine. In twenty years, no one will be able to surpass you. Take care of yourself!"

Later, Master Yang-shan told everyone, "Kuang-yung is a living Buddha."

What is the meaning of this *kung-an*? If someone asks us to describe what a person looks like, it would be very complicated to provide a response. For if people look like one thing, there are bound to be certain things that they will not look like.

As the *Diamond Sutra* states: "All forms are delusive ... If one sees that all forms are not forms, one will see the *Tathāgata*."

What is empty space like? Empty space has no form, and yet, there is no form that empty space is not like. It is because empty space has no form that it can contain everything and can resemble everything.

Master Yang-shan and Master Kuang-yung were discussing what the Master looks like if he neither looks like a donkey nor like a Buddha. Well, he looks like himself. Only when we see our true nature will we become one with empty space. If we forget the distinction between an ordinary person and a Buddha, then we will see the truth of formlessness.

A Pearl Wrapped in Rags

One day, Prime Minister P'ei-hsiu went to Ta-an Temple and asked the monks, "Buddha's ten great disciples were all outstanding in different areas. In what area was Rahula[4] outstanding?"

Everyone thought that it was an easy question, so they all answered, "He was outstanding in esoteric practices."

P'ei-hsiu was not satisfied with this answer, so he asked, "Are there any Ch'an masters present?"

Ch'an Master Lung-ya was working in the vegetable garden at the time, so the monks asked him to join them. P'ei-hsiu repeated the question, "In what area was Rahula outstanding?"

"I don't know!" Master Lung-ya answered without any hesitation.

P'ei-hsiu was pleased, immediately prostrated himself before Lung-ya, and praised him, exclaiming, "A pearl wrapped in rags!"

Everyone had heard that Rahula was outstanding in esoteric practices. Since they were esoteric, how could the monks claim that they knew what they were? Hence, P'ei-hsiu felt that Master Lung-ya's response "I don't know!" was much more legitimate. In contrast, the response made by the other monks was not based on real knowledge, only on hearsay.

If we know something, then we know it. If we don't know it, then we don't. Regardless of whether we know it, knowledge is not something we should pretend to possess.

A Monk Named "Water-drop"

One day, Ch'an Master I-shan was taking a bath. The water was too hot, so he called for one of his disciples to bring a bucket of cold water.

A disciple brought a bucket of water and added some of the cold water to the hot water to cool it. After cooling the bath water, there was some water left in the bucket, so he just threw it away.

The Master was not very pleased with this, so he said, "Why are you so wasteful? Everything in this world has its use. Things only differ in their kinds of use. Take even one drop of water for example. If you give it to the flowers or the trees, then not only will the flowers and trees be happy, the water drop itself will not lose its value. A single drop of water is very valuable. You should not waste it."

After listening to the Master, the disciple changed his name to "Water-drop."

Later, when Water-drop started to teach Buddhism, people asked him, "What is the most virtuous thing in the world?"

"Water drop," he answered.

"Empty space can contain all things. What can contain empty space?"

"Water drop!"

Master Water-drop was already in harmony with the water drop. The whole universe was his mind. Thus, one drop of water can encompass limitless time and space.

How much merit do we have in this world? There is a limitation. No matter how wealthy we are, when we have depleted its supply, we will be penniless. Money, love, life—the amount of each of these things that we possess can be compared to a savings account in a bank. If we squander the merits that we have, the account will soon be exhausted. Therefore, we should use our merits sparingly and should not be wasteful. Not even a single drop of water should be wasted. Although a drop of water is very small, the vast ocean is made up of water drops.

Meditate on Stinky Urine

Ch'an Master Ts'ung-yüeh went to visit Ch'an Master Shou-chih. After they had chatted briefly, Master Shou-chih began to criticize Ts'ung-yüeh, "Although you are the Head Monk of Tao-wu Shan, you talk just like a drunkard!"

Ts'ung-yüeh turned red with embarrassment and replied, "Please be compassionate and teach me!"

Master Shou-chih asked him, "Have you ever gone to study with

Ch'an Master Fa-ch'ang?"

"I have read his teachings and taken them to heart, so I did not go to study with him in person."

Master Shou-chih asked again, "Did you go to study with Ch'an Master K'e-wen?"

Scornfully, Ts'ung-yüeh replied, "K'e-wen? He is a crazy man! He drags around a rag that smells of stinky urine. He is no Ch'an master!"

Master Shou-chih said solemnly, "Ch'an is right there! Go and meditate on stinky urine!"

Ts'ung-yüeh took Master Shou-chih's advice and went to study with Master K'e-wen. He finally attained realization and returned to thank Master Shou-chih.

Master Shou-chih asked him, "What have you learned from Master K'e-wen?"

Ts'ung-yüeh answered respectfully, "If it was not for your advice, my life would have been wasted. So I came back to say thank you!"

Master Shou-chih said, "Thank me for what? You should thank the stinky urine!"

Average people always make the mistake of judging others by their outward appearances. Where is Ch'an? Ch'an is not necessarily found in what appears to be pleasant or beautiful. The eye of wisdom can see Ch'an even in "a rag that smells of stinky urine." This is why the lotus grows from the mud, while gold and precious stones are found to be embedded in rocks.

Please Take Care

One day, when Ch'an Master Ling-hsün was studying with Ch'an Master Kuei-tzung, he suddenly decided to leave and went to Master Kuei-tzung to take his leave.

Kuei-tzung said, "Where are you going?"

Ling-hsün answered, "Back to the mountains."

"You have studied here for thirteen years. Now that you are leaving, I should tell you the essence of the Dharma. When you have finished packing, come and see me again."

Ling-hsün followed the Master's instructions, leaving his luggage outside the door as he went in to see Master Kuei-tzung.

Master Kuei-tzung beckoned to him, "Come over here!"

Ling-hsün did as he was instructed.

The Master said gently, "The weather is cold. Please take care of yourself during the journey."

Upon hearing this, Ling-hsün became enlightened.

What is Master Kuei-tzung's "essence of the Dharma"? The mind of compassion, the *bodhicitta*, and the mind of *prajñā* are all the minds of Ch'an.

When we study the Dharma, if we give up halfway before we are through, we are not accepting responsibility for our actions.

The statement "The weather is cold" demonstrates Master Kuei-tzung's caring nature. Others care for us; how can we not care for ourselves? "Please take care of yourself during the journey"—these few words of encouragement allowed Ling-hsün to recognize his own self.

Sometimes, despite lectures on thousands of sutras, we still have not touched even the fringes of Ch'an. Other times, a few words or an unintentional action can lead one to see one's true face.

The compassionate care shown by Master Kuei-tzung came from the fact that he had been living with and instructing Ling-hsün for thirteen years, while Ling-hsün's realization was due to the ripening of his own practice. According to a Chinese saying: "If the rice is not cooked, do not open the lid. If the egg has not hatched, do not crack it open." When one is ready, one is ready. Enlightenment is not something that can be forced.

Compassion

Three brothers, although not monastics, were very devout Buddhists. They were traveling together to visit different Ch'an masters.

One day, they stayed with a family of seven children whose father had just passed away. The next day, as the three brothers were just about to leave, the youngest brother told the other two, "You go ahead with your travels. I've decided to stay."

The two older brothers were not pleased with the youngest brother's decision and left angrily.

It would not be easy for the widow to bring up seven young children, so the youngest brother's decision to stay was very helpful. Later, the widow wanted to marry him, but he said, "Your husband has just died. It would not be proper for us to get married so soon. You should remain in mourning for three years before we discuss marriage."

Three years later, the widow proposed to him again. He replied, "If I marry you now, I would be disrespectful to your husband. For three years, let me be in mourning for him."

After another three years, the widow proposed to him once more. He replied, "For the sake of our future happiness, let us mourn for your husband together for three more years before getting married."

Nine years after the husband passed away, the children had grown up. The youngest brother now felt that his mission had been fulfilled, and he left the widow to continue on with his spiritual pursuit.

Although the youngest brother had not received lessons from a Ch'an master, he nonetheless was practicing Ch'an by helping the widow and her children. He was not only able to overcome worldly temptations but can also transform defilements into purity.

Ch'an, if applied in our daily lives, would be like a ship in the sea of suffering. It would be like a bright light in the darkness. At the same instant, it would serve as true medicine for the illnesses of our world.

Where Is the Buddha Now?

Once, Emperor Shun-tzung asked Ch'an Master Ju-man, "From where did the Buddha come? Where did he go? If we say the Buddha dwells in this world eternally, then where is the Buddha now?"

Master Ju-man answered, "The Buddha came from the eternal[5] and returned to the eternal. His true nature[6] is one with empty space. He dwells in a place where there is no-mind.[7] The mindful merges with the mindless. The dwelling merges with the non-dwelling. He came and went away for the sake of all beings. The pure sea of true nature is his profound body that abides eternally. The wise should contemplate this carefully and not permit any doubts to arise!"

Emperor Shun-tzung was not convinced and said, "The Buddha was born in a palace and passed away between two śāla [teak wood] trees. He taught for forty-nine years and said that he did not expound a word of Dharma. The mountains, the rivers and oceans, the sun and moon, heaven and Earth—all will cease to exist when the time comes. Who said there is no birth and no death? The wise should be able to grasp a clear understanding of this."

Then Master Ju-man explained, "The essence of the Buddha is non-being, and only the deluded will make distinctions. His true nature is one with empty space and will neither experience birth nor death. When the right conditions are present, the Buddha will be born. When the right conditions cease to exist, the Buddha will pass away. He teaches beings everywhere, just as the moon reflects on all water. He is neither permanent nor is he impermanent; he had neither an origin nor an extinction; he was neither born, nor did he ever die. When one sees the place of no-mind, then there is no Dharma to speak of."

Pleased with the response, Emperor Shun-tzung became more respectful toward the Master.

People often say, "Amitābha Buddha is in the Western Pure Land. The Medicine Buddha is in the Eastern Pure Land. Where is Śākyamuni Buddha?" Śākyamuni Buddha is in the Land of Perpetual Peace and Glory.

When a Ch'an practitioner is asked to explain these kinds of questions, the ensuing discussion can be very vivacious. Because we perceive with our minds, we see the world of birth and death. This is the realm of the Buddha's manifestation as a physical being. If we perceive with no-mind, then we will see the world of no birth and no death. This is the true nature. No-mind is the Ch'an mind. Only through the use of our Ch'an minds will we be able to discern the true whereabouts of the Buddha.

"When the right conditions are present, the Buddha will be born. When the right conditions cease to exist, the Buddha will pass away." This passing away is not death, but rather, the state of nirvana. In the Land of Perpetual Peace and Glory, there are no distinctions, no suffering, and no relativity. It is in the world of bliss that one will find true bliss.

Sugar Cookie

A monk went to study with Ch'an Master Tao-ming. The Master asked the monk, "What kind of Buddhist teachings have you read?"

The monk replied, "I have read the Yogācāra teaching."

The Master asked, "Can you lecture on this subject?"

The monk declared, "I dare not."

Master Tao-ming picked up a sugar cookie, broke it in two, and asked, "The three worlds are nothing but the mind's manifestation; the ten thousand dharmas all arise from consciousness. What do you say to that?"

The monk was dumbfounded.

Tao-ming persisted, "Should this be called a sugar cookie, or should it not be called a sugar cookie?"

The monk was perspiring now and answered nervously, "It should be called a sugar cookie."

The Master then asked a novice who was standing nearby, "A sugar cookie has been broken into two pieces—what do you have to say about it?"

The novice answered without hesitation, "The two pieces remain in one mind."

Master Tao-ming continued, "What do you call it?"

The novice replied, "A sugar cookie."

Master Tao-ming laughed heartily and said, "You can also lecture on the teachings of Yogācāra!"

The method and direction of studying Yogācāra differ from that of studying Ch'an. Yogācāra's idealism emphasizes understanding and analysis, whereas Ch'an does not. A Ch'an adept aims directly at the mind, attaining Buddhahood by seeing one's own nature. Ch'an masters use humor in their speech and treat people with kindness. They do not like to present a stern face. Sometimes, when they talk about east, they are actually pointing west. Sometimes, when they strike or scold a student, they are actually expressing their loving kindness.

Whereas a scholar of Yogācāra employs ample verbal explanation to expound on the doctrine of idealism, a Ch'an practitioner only has to say "A sugar cookie," and the underlying implications

are conveyed. This alone is sufficient to express the meaning of "The three worlds are nothing but the mind's manifestation; the ten thousand dharmas all arise from consciousness."

Hui-k'o Pacifying His Mind

Shen-kuang Hui-k'o traveled thousands of miles to Shao-lin Temple at Sung Shan, where he paid his respects to Bodhidharma, hoping to hear his teachings and to become his disciple.

Since Bodhidharma was meditating with his face towards the wall, he paid no attention to Hui-k'o, who stood motionless outside the door. It was snowing heavily, and after a long time had passed, the snow had reached Hui-k'o's knees. Impressed by Hui-k'o's sincerity, Bodhidharma inquired, "You have been standing in the snow for quite a long time. What do you want?"

Hui-k'o replied, "I would just like to beg the Master to open the Gate of Truth so as to benefit all beings."

"The wonderful way of the Buddhas may not be attained even through aeons of great effort, not even by practicing the impossible and tolerating the intolerable. With your impertinent mind, you are just wasting your time in wanting to attain the true teaching."

After hearing this teaching, Hui-k'o cut off his arm.

Bodhidharma said, "Buddhas forget about their own bodies for the sake of Dharma. Now that you have cut off your arm, what are you looking for?"

"My mind is not pacified. Please help me pacify my mind!"

"Bring me your mind! I will pacify it for you!"

Startled, Hui-k'o exclaimed, "I can't find my mind!"

Bodhidharma smiled and said, "I have already pacified your mind."

At that instant, Hui-k'o became enlightened.

Suffering is originally empty, while negative karma originally lacks a self-nature. Only when the consciousness is still and when there are no more delusory thoughts will we attain perfect enlightenment. When we can maintain a true mind that is not confused, the Buddha-nature will shine through instantaneously.

A Twenty-Percent Discount

A son went to ask Ch'an Master Fo-kuang to perform chanting for his deceased father. Because the son was worried that it might be too expensive, he repeatedly asked about the cost. The Master was not pleased with the son's stinginess and replied, "It will cost ten ounces of silver to chant the *Amitābha Sutra*."

The son exclaimed, "Ten ounces of silver? That's too expensive! How about giving me a twenty-percent discount? Eight ounces, okay?"

The Master agreed.

As the chanting was about to end, the Master murmured, "Buddhas and bodhisattvas of the ten directions, please transfer all the merits from this chanting to the deceased person so that he can go to the Eastern Pure Land."

The son protested, "Master, I've only heard of people going to the Western Pure Land, but I have never heard of the Eastern Pure Land."

The Master said, "It takes ten ounces of silver to transfer your father to the Western Pure Land. You insisted on having a twenty-percent discount, so your father can only go to the Eastern Pure Land."

The son replied, "In that case, I will give you two more ounces. Please transfer my father to the Western Pure Land."

Suddenly, the father spoke from his coffin, "You scrooge! Just because you wanted to save two ounces of silver, you made me go back and forth from the East to the West. Do you know how tiring that is?"

Buddhist teaching is not a commodity, so we should not attempt to strike a bargain with it as we might in doing business. According to a Buddhist sutra: "The merit attained for doing a good deed depends on the intention of the doer and the virtue of the receiver." This simply implies that if we give ten dollars to someone, the virtue achieved will be far greater if this person uses it in a beneficial manner as opposed to the person using it in a non-productive or destructive manner.

Buddhism is priceless. We cannot determine how much merit will be gained based on its monetary contributions but can determine its merit on the level of sincerity.

A Ch'an Master's Tears

One day, Ch'an Master K'ung-yeh was traveling on the road and met some bandits who wanted to rob him.

Tears fell from the Master's eyes.

The bandits started laughing and exclaimed, "What a coward!"

Master K'ung-yeh then said, "Don't think that I'm crying because I'm afraid of you. I'm not even afraid of birth and death. I feel sorry for you young people. You are strong and healthy, yet instead of doing things that are beneficial for others, you hurt people by robbing them. Of course, what you are doing is not acceptable and cannot be tolerated by society. What is worse is that you will all go to hell and suffer great pain. I am so worried about you that I cannot restrain myself and am shedding tears for you."

The bandits were moved and decided to give up their evil ways.

There are many kinds of tears. There are tears of sorrow, tears of happiness, and tears of compassion. Master K'ung-yeh's tears were tears of compassion, flowing from the compassionate Ch'an mind which cleanses the world of its defilements.

I-hsiu Sunning His 'Sutra'

One day, Ch'an Master I-hsiu, who was living on Pi-rui Shan, saw a vast crowd of Buddhist followers swarming up the mountain because the monastics at the temple were sunning their sutras.[8]

There was a superstition that if the wind blew over the sutras, it could also blow away troubles and impart wisdom. Hence, many people hurried to Pi-rui Shan in search of these benefits. Upon hearing this, Master I-hsiu said, "In that case, I shall also sun my 'sutra'!" He took off his clothes and laid out under the sun. Some lay followers who saw I-hsiu were appalled by his behavior.

Later, the monks of the temple learned of the incident and told I-hsiu that he should not be so crude.

I-hsiu then explained his actions by saying, "The sutras that you are sunning are dead, so they have book worms. The 'sutra' that I am sunning is alive; it can teach the Dharma, work, and eat. A wise person should know which kind of 'sutra' is more valuable!"

Although I-hsiu's behavior seems outrageous, it implies that wisdom must be sought from within oneself.

Sutras are printed on paper, but only our true minds behold the real Dharma. Why not look after our minds instead of looking after a bundle of papers? The most precious sutra is not printed on paper but is contained in our minds. The "sutras" in our minds generate all dharmas.

A True Attendant

One day, Ch'an Master Shih-t'i saw his attendant heading toward the dining hall while carrying a bowl. He asked, "Where are you going?"

The attendant answered, "To the dining hall!"

Master Shih-t'i reproached him by saying, "I know that you are going to the dining hall."

"If the Master knows, then why did you ask me?"

Shih-t'i replied, "I am asking about your duty."

The attendant answered, "If the Master asks about my duty, then I am really going to the dining hall."

Shih-t'i said approvingly, "You are truly my attendant!"

What is our duty? It is to perceive our nature, to be liberated from birth and death, to return to our homes.

Ch'an permeates a Ch'an practitioner's life. Eating is Ch'an. Sleeping is Ch'an. Walking, standing, sitting, lying down, chopping firewood, and carrying water are all Ch'an. Ch'an is not just limited to the way we conduct ourselves in our everyday living, but it also encompasses all phenomena of the universe.

If we shoulder our responsibilities and refrain from seeking things that are not rightfully ours, then this is the mind of Ch'an.

Looking at You with Blinking Eyes

Ch'an Master Yang-shan was trying to test Ch'an Master Chih-hsien's understanding of Ch'an. Hence, he said to him, "Dharma brother, what have you gained from meditation lately?"

Chih-hsien answered, "Last year, I was poor but was not really poor. This year, I am poor and am really poor. Last year, I was poor, but I still had somewhere to stand. This year, I am so poor that I don't even have anywhere to stand."

Yang-shan said to him in reply, "Dharma brother, I admit that you have already penetrated into the *Tathāgata*'s Ch'an[9], but you have not yet entered the door of the Patriarchs' Ch'an[10]."

In reply, Chih-hsien recited a verse:

> I have a teaching,
> Looking at you with blinking eyes.
> If you don't understand,
> Don't call yourself a student of the Path.

Yang-shan was very content with Chih-hsien's progress and went to report the incident to their teacher, Ch'an Master Kuei-shan. Yang-shan said, "How exciting! Dharma brother Chih-hsien has already entered the Patriarchs' Ch'an."

Both Chih-hsien and Yang-shan were disciples of Ch'an Master Pai-chang.

During the T'ang dynasty, after the time of the Sixth Patriarch, Hui-nêng, Ch'an underwent great changes. The first major change was initiated by Ch'an Master Ma-tsu Tao-i, who established forest monasteries to accept Ch'an practitioners from the ten directions so that they could practice as a community.

Later, Ch'an Master Pai-chang Huai-hai established the "Pure Rules" so that the monastic community could dwell in harmony. His disciples disseminated his teachings and taught that one should not depend on written or spoken language, but instead, rely on the everyday mind, which was the Path to Buddhahood.

Hitting and shouting became accepted methods of teaching. The exchanges between teacher and student were concise and quick.

These became the essence of the Chinese Patriarchs' Ch'an, which differed considerably from the *Tathāgata*'s Ch'an of India.

"I am so poor that I don't even have anywhere to stand" simply implies the non-clinging to the *Tathāgata*'s Ch'an, while "Looking at you with blinking eyes" would be a representation of the Patriarchs' Ch'an.

Whose Fault Is It?

A lay Buddhist was taking a walk by the river when he saw a boatman pushing a boat towards the river so that he could take some passengers across.

A Ch'an master happened to pass by. The lay Buddhist approached the Master and asked, "Master, that boatman killed many little crabs and shrimps while he was pushing the boat in the river. Is this the fault of the passengers, or is it the fault of the boatman?"

The Master retorted without hesitation, "It is neither the fault of the passengers nor the fault of the boatman!"

The lay Buddhist did not understand, so he asked again, "If it is the fault of neither, then whose fault is it?"

The Master replied sharply, "It is your fault!"

The boatman had to make a living. The passengers had to cross the river. The crabs and shrimps had to have a place to hide themselves. Therefore, whose fault was it? It was the fault of all three. At the same instance, it was also not their fault, because all three of them had "no-mind."

According to Buddhist scriptures: "Faults, which are originally nonexistent, are created by the mind. When the mind does not give rise to discriminating thoughts, no fault will arise." When there is "no-mind," how can any faults be committed? Even when someone committed a wrong doing, it would be committed unintentionally. Faults were created by the discriminating thoughts of the lay Buddhist. No wonder the Master blamed him!

The Oil Peddler

One day, while Ch'an Master Chao-chou was on his way to T'ung-cheng County, he met Ch'an Master Ta-t'ung of T'ou-tzŭ Shan and asked, "Are you the Master of T'ou-tzŭ Shan?"

Ta-t'ung waved his hands and exclaimed, "Salt, tea, and oil. Please buy some!"

Chao-chou ignored him and quickly proceeded to the temple. Master Ta-t'ung followed behind and arrived at the temple with a bottle of oil in his hand. Chao-chou said to him scornfully, "I have heard of the great name of Master Ta-t'ung of T'ou-tzŭ Shan for a long time. However, I only see an oil peddler."

Ta-t'ung retorted, "I also have heard that Chao-chou is a Ch'an master, but in fact, he is no different from an average person. You only see the oil peddler and do not see T'ou- tzŭ[11]."

Chao-chou asked, "Why do you say that I am an average person? What is T'ou-tzŭ?"

Master Ta-t'ung lifted the oil bottle and shouted, "Oil! Oil!"

"What is T'ou-tzŭ?" asked Chao-chou, to which the only response was "Oil! Oil!" Rice, salt, tea, and oil—the staples of Chinese life—such is the teaching of Master T'ou-tzŭ.

I Am No Buddha

A scholar went to live in a temple. Thinking that he was clever, he often debated with Ch'an Master Chao-chou.

One day, he asked the Master, "The Buddha was very compassionate. When he was helping sentient beings, he had always tried to fulfill their wishes. Whatever they wished for, Buddha would try to satisfy them. Is this correct?"

Master Chao-chou exclaimed, "Yes!"

The scholar continued, "I wish very much to have the cane in your hand, but I don't know whether my wish can be granted."

Master Chao-chou refused by saying, "A gentleman does not take by force what others like. Do you understand?"

The scholar countered, "I am no gentleman."

"Nor am I a Buddha!" shouted Chao-chou.

Another time, as the scholar was sitting in meditation, Chao-chou passed by. The scholar looked at the Master but paid no attention to him. Chao-chou reprimanded him by saying, "Young man, why don't you stand up when you see an elder?"

He replied, "Sitting is the same as standing!"

Master Chao-chou slapped him across the face.

Infuriated, the young scholar demanded an explanation.

Master Chao-chou said gently, "Slapping you is the same as not slapping you."

The scholar was an intellectual, while the Ch'an master was someone who had already realized the Truth. An intellectual cannot be compared with someone who has attained realization—especially not with someone like Master Chao-chou, whose Ch'an was vivacious, swift, pure, and meticulous.

Chao-chou was not so attached to his staff that he refused to give it up. He simply did not like the way the scholar asked for it.

Chao-chou's action of slapping the scholar across the face and his remark "Slapping you is the same as not slapping you" should serve as a lesson to those who flaunt their Ch'an study without having realized the Truth!

I Have a Tongue Too

When Ch'an Master Kuang-hui Yüan-lien first started to learn Ch'an, he went to Ch'an Master Chen-chüeh. During the day, he worked in the kitchen, and in the evening, he chanted sutras.

One day, Master Chen-chüeh asked him, "What sutra are you chanting now?"

Yüan-lien answered, "The *Vimalakīrti Sutra*."

Chen-chüeh inquired, "The Sutra is here. Where is Vimalakīrti?"

Yüan-lien did not know how to answer, hence he asked Master

Chen-chüeh, "Where is Vimalakīrti?"

Chen-chüeh exclaimed, "Whether I know or not, I cannot tell you!"

Yüan-lien felt so ashamed that he left his master and went to learn from over fifty other Ch'an masters. Yet, he could not attain realization.

One day, he went to visit Hsing-nien and asked, "I am going to a treasure mountain. What should I do if I leave empty-handed?"

Master Hsing-nien declared, "Dig out the treasure that is within yourself!"

Yüan-lien attained realization instantly and said, "I have no doubts about the tongues of Ch'an masters."

Hsing-nien queried, "Why?"

Yüan-lien responded, "I have a tongue too."

Hsing-nien was elated and said, "You have already realized the essence of Ch'an."

Everyone has a tongue, but not everyone knows its wonderful function. The tongue can be used for speech. One word can save a country. One word also can destroy a country. It depends on whether you know how to use your tongue. Some use their tongues to do good, while others use their tongues to do evil. Does everyone understand a Ch'an master's tongue?

Thinking of Not Thinking

One day, while Ch'an Master Wei-yen was meditating, a monk walked by, saw him, and inquired, "You are sitting here as still as a rock. What are you thinking?"

The Master answered, "I am thinking of not thinking."

The monk continued, "How do you do that?"

Wei-yen responded, "By not thinking."

In reality, thinking and not thinking seem mutually contradictory, yet there is an underlying implication. Ch'an is not merely a matter of understanding words. In the teaching of Ch'an, words are considered obstacles to realization. Nonetheless, through understanding words, the essence that cannot be verbally communicated

can be grasped. The true taste of Ch'an can only be experienced
when one has given up one's clinging to intellectual understanding.

The Dharma Is Not Dual

A Confucian scholar by the name of Han Yü angered the emperor by
writing admonitions, advising him not to receive the Buddha's relics.
Therefore, he was exiled to Ch'ao-chou.

While there, Han Yü went to visit Ch'an Master Pao-t'ung and
asked, "Master, how old are you?"

The Master held up his rosary and queried, "Do you know?"

Han Yü declared, "No, I do not!"

Pao-t'ung added, "Day and night, 108."

Han Yü could not figure out why he did not understand what the
Master had said, and so he left.

The next day, Han Yü returned. Meeting the head monk of the
temple, he told him about the conversation that he had with Master
Pao-t'ung and asked the head monk what it meant.

After listening to the account, the head monk tapped his teeth three
times. Han Yü grew even more baffled. He went to see Master
Pao-t'ung and asked him again, "Master, how old are you?"

Master Pao-t'ung also tapped his teeth three times.

Suddenly, Han Yü seemed to understand and said, "Ah! The
Dharma is not dual."

Master Pao-t'ung asked, "Why?"

Han Yü answered, "The head monk gave the same answer you just
did."

Master Pao-t'ung mumbled to himself and said, "The teaching of
Buddhism and Confucianism are not dual. You and I are the same!"

Han Yü finally understood and later became a Buddhist.

Han Yü inquired about the Master's age. However, physical age is
not relevant. What is important is to become one with Nature. The
mind and the Buddha should become one. Buddhists and Confucians should come to a mutual understanding.

When the Master showed his rosary and said, "Day and night,

108," he meant that time was limited, and there was no need for Buddhists and Confucians to quarrel. The two should cooperate and work together.

Seeing and Not Seeing

After listening to the views of Ch'an Master Shou-hsün, Ch'an Master Fo-chien said, "It is a pity that such a shiny pearl has been picked up by this crazy fellow." He continued by quoting the poem of Ch'an Master Ling-yün, "'Ever since I saw the peach flower, I have never had a doubt.' Why did Ling-yün have no doubts?"

Shou-hsün immediately replied, "Do not say that Ling-yün have no doubts; even today, we cannot find a doubt anywhere."

Fo-chien asked, "Hsüan-sha said: 'This noble truth is very true, but I cannot understand it thoroughly!' What was it that he could not understand thoroughly?"

Shou-hsün answered politely, "We can see that Ch'an Master Hsüan-sha had very good intentions." He continued by reciting the following verse:

> Looking at the sky all day without lifting
>   one's head,
> Raising one's eyes only when the peach
>   flower blooms;
> Even if you have a net that covers the sky,
> When you break through the tightly shut
>   gate, you will be home free.

Master Fo-chien felt that Shou-hsün was enlightened, but Master Yüan-wu did not think along the same line. He wanted to observe Master Shou-hsün, so he traveled with him. When they came to the side of a lake, Master Yüan-wu pushed Shou-hsün into the water and asked, "Before Niu-t'ou Fa-jung met the Fourth Patriarch, what was he like?"

Shou-hsün answered, "When the lake is deep, fishes will gather."

Yüan-wu continued, "What about after they met?"

Shou-hsün responded, "The tall trees catch the wind."

"What about when they both met and had not met?"

Shou-hsün answered, "The extended foot is on the withdrawn foot."

Master Yüan-wu was greatly impressed by Shou-hsün's responses and became convinced that Shou-hsün was truly enlightened.

A Ch'an practitioner's realization can be tested. Shou-hsün was repeatedly tested; only then was he recognized as an enlightened Ch'an master.

Not Allowed to Be the Teacher

Ch'an Master Tou-shuai Ts'ung-yüeh had great respect for Ch'an Master Ch'ing-su.

Once, Ts'ung-yüeh had some lichee with him and was passing by Ch'ing-su's window. He stopped and said politely, "Master, these fruits are from Kiangsi, my home town. Have some."

Ch'ing-su gladly accepted, saying, "Ever since my master passed away, I have not had any lichees for a long time."

Ts'ung-yüeh asked, "Who was your master?"

"Master Tz'ŭ-ming. I was his subordinate for thirteen years."

Ts'ung-yüeh was surprised to hear this and exclaimed, "After being on his staff for thirteen years, you must have inherited his teaching."

He then offered all his lichees to Master Ch'ing-su.

Ch'ing-su said gratefully, "Because I have not accumulated enough merit, my master instructed me not to pass on what I have learned from him. Now I see that you are very sincere and for the sake of the friendship that we have made through these lichees, I shall make an exception. Tell me, what have you realized?"

Ts'ung-yüeh told Ch'ing-su who then instructed, "Both the Buddha and the devil exist in this world. At the moment of liberation, one should enter Buddha's path, not the devil's path."

After confirming Ts'ung-yüeh's realization, Master Ch'ing-su warned him, "Today, I have confirmed your realization so that you can attain true liberation. However, you should not tell people that you have inherited my teaching. Master Chen-ch'ing K'e-wen is your teacher."

To learn the Dharma, we first have to create the right conditions. Even lichee can contribute to our enlightenment. "The Dharma can only be sought through respect." Ts'ung-yüeh's respect for his elders contributed to his realization.

Gratitude was also a virtue of the ancients. Out of gratitude for the gift of a few lichees, Master Ch'ing-su confirmed Ts'ung-yüeh's realization.

Ch'ing-su's warning that Ts'ung-yüeh should regard Master Chen-ch'ing K'e-wen as his teacher demonstrated the respect and trust that Ch'an masters have for each other.

The Iron Cow Jumped over Hsin-lo

After reading *The Record of Tung-shan*, the attendant of Ch'an Master Fa-ch'ing was deeply touched and said, "It is really odd how detached the ancients were regarding birth and death."

Master Fa-ch'ing answered, "When I pass away, remember to call my name. If I come back to life, that means I have been liberated from birth and death. There is nothing odd about it." The Master then wrote a verse:

> On the fifth day of the fifth month,
> The four great elements shall leave this owner.
> My white bones shall drift with the wind,
> No benefactor's land will be wasted.

On the fifth day of the fifth month of the lunar calendar, Master Fa-ch'ing gave all his clothing and belongings to his attendant for distribution to the other monks. At midnight, the Master sat cross-legged; both his heart beat and breathing stopped. Remembering the Master's instructions, the attendant called out, "Master! Master!"

Finally, Master Fa-ch'ing opened his eyes and asked, "What?"

"Master, why don't you put on your clothes before you leave?"

Fa-ch'ing declared, "When I first came, I did not bring anything!"

The attendant insisted on helping the Master put on his clothes. "One cannot even leave a little bit for one's posterity."

The attendant asked, "What are you going to do about it?"
Fa-ch'ing said, "Let it be," and chanted:

> Seventy-three years passed like a flash of
>   lightning,
> Before departing, I leave you a last message.
> When the iron cow jumped over Hsin-lo[12],
> It smashed the empty space into seven or
>   eight pieces.

Then he passed away.

**Ch'an masters are subject to birth and death; however, they feel at
ease when facing either one. Empty-handed they came into the
world, and empty-handed they shall depart from it. This is true
liberation.**

A General's Repentance

One day, Ch'an Master Meng-ch'uang decided to take the ferry across
the river. After the ferry had left the landing, a general carrying a sword
and whip, suddenly arrived, and shouted, "Wait! Take me over!"

Almost everyone on the ferry agreed that it should not go back, so
the boatman shouted, "Wait for the next ferry!"

Master Meng-ch'uang then said to the boatman, "We are still very
close to shore. Go back and take him over."

Seeing that it was a monk who spoke, the boatman turned around
and picked up the general. When the general got on the ferry, he stood
next to Master Meng-ch'uang and struck him with his whip, shouting,
"Get up, give me your seat!"

Soon, blood was dripping from the Master's head. He got up
without saying a word. Everyone was frightened and did not dare speak.
Although the general knew that he was wrong, he was too stubborn to
apologize.

When the ferry reached the other shore, Master Meng-ch'uang got
off and went to the edge of the river to wash off the blood on his face.

The general felt great remorse for what he had done. He went up to Master Meng-ch'uang, knelt in front of him, and said, "Master, I am very sorry!"

Master Meng-ch'uang said gently, "Don't worry about it. People traveling away from home sometimes may feel the blues."

What is the most potent thing on Earth? Tolerance. The Buddha once said, "A Buddhist practitioner who cannot tolerate slander, abuse, ridicule, and treat them as sweet dew is not a person of strength."

Violence can inspire fear in people but cannot earn their respect. Only tolerance can touch the hearts of the stubborn.

Everything Is Already at Hand!

While traveling one day, Ch'an Master Fa-yen Wen-i was stranded by a snow storm and had to stay with Ch'an Master Kuei-ch'en.

After a few days, the snow storm stopped, so Fa-yen decided to leave and continue with his journey.

While Master Kuei-ch'en was walking with Fa-yen to the main gate, he pointed at a big rock by the roadside and said, "You have always said, 'The three worlds are nothing but the mind's manifestation and the ten thousand dharmas all arise from consciousness.' Is this rock inside or outside of your mind?"

Spontaneously, Fa-yen answered, "According to the teaching of Yogācāra, there are no dharmas outside of the mind. Of course, the rock must be inside of the mind."

Master Kuei-ch'en seized this opportunity and asked, "Are you not traveling? Then why do you keep a chunk of rock in your mind?"

Fa-yen did not know how to respond, so he decided to stay in search of the answer to this question. He worked on the question every day and gave different answers to Master Kuei-ch'en. But no matter what point of view he used to tackle the question, Master Kuei-ch'en always disagreed and declared, "Buddhism is not like this!"

Finally, Fa-yen sighed, "I have run out of words and ideas."

Master Kuei-ch'en exclaimed, "If we are talking about Buddhism, then everything is already at hand!"

Master Fa-yen attained realization at that instant. Later, he established the Fa-yen School of Ch'an Buddhism in China.

To add horns to a horse or to add an extra head to the head is unnecessary. "If we are talking about Buddhism, then everything is already at hand." What a beautiful and wonderful state of mind! The burdens that we carry around in our minds are not just chunks of rocks. The burdens of money, fame, love, and life are so heavy that we can hardly breathe. When right and wrong, honor and dishonor, suffering and happiness are added, the burdens become even more unbearable. If we understand that "everything is already at hand," then why should we worry about whether things are created solely by our minds or by our consciousness?

Life or Death, Let It Be!

Before Ch'an Master Pao-fu passed away he told his disciples, "I have been feeling weak lately. I suspect that it is almost time for me to go."

Upon hearing this, some of his disciples said, "Master, you still look very healthy."

Others implored, "Master, we still need your guidance," while some urged, "Master, please stay for the sake of all beings."

One disciple asked, "Master, when it is time for you to go, will you go or will you stay?"

Master Pao-fu asked, "Which do you think would be better?"

The disciple answered without hesitation, "Whether it is life or death, let it be!"

The Master started laughing, "When did you steal the words that I was going to use?"

Upon saying this, Pao-fu passed away.

To the average person, life is something to be happy about, whereas death is lamentable. To a realized Buddhist practitioner life is not something to be happy about, nor is death a cause for lament. Life and death are two sides of the same coin. The cycle of life and

death is part of the law of Nature.

Many Ch'an practitioners have said that life and death have nothing to do with them. A Ch'an practitioner is neither greedy for life nor afraid of death but regards both life and death with a liberated attitude.

Silence Is Better than Chatter

During the Five dynasties (907-960 C.E.), King Liu of Hou Han insisted on inviting Ch'an Master Yün-men and all the monastics of his temple to spend their summer retreat at the palace.

Lectures were delivered every day. Ladies of the court and ministers were very eager to listen to the teachings and were also anxious to ask questions. Everyone was happily involved in this festive exchange of Buddhism except for Master Yün-men, who meditated quietly by himself. No one dared to disturb him.

An officer saw Yün-men and asked him some questions. Yün-men responded with silence. The officer was not offended but respected Yün-men even more. He wrote the following poem and posted it:

> To practice with great wisdom is true Ch'an,
> In which silence is better than chatter.
> Clever talk about the truth is inferior to the
> silence of Ch'an.

Ch'an masters are like floating clouds and wild cranes. They sometimes live in forests and sometimes by the water. Carrying only their three robes[13] and one bowl, they live in accordance with their surroundings, unmoved by wealth, gain, or power.

Master Yün-men's silence was like the sound of thunder. If we can understand the Buddha's teaching through silence, then we have obtained a glimmer of Ch'an.

The Head Monk

For twenty years, the position of head monk at Ling-shu Temple had been vacant. When people asked Ch'an Master Ling-shu Ju-min about the position, he replied, "Our head monk has just been born."

Later, when someone else asked the same question, Ling-shu answered, "Our head monk is tending his cow."

Still later, when people inquired about the head monk, Ling-shu replied, "Our head monk is away cultivating himself through travel."

No one really understood what the Master meant.

One day, the Master ordered his disciples to beat the drum, strike the bell, and instructed everyone to go to the main gate to welcome the head monk. Everyone was puzzled. When Yün-men arrived, Master Ju-min asked him to assume the position of head monk.

From that time onward, people began to believe that Master Ling-shu had the power to know the past as well as the future.

Soon afterward, King Liu of Hou Han was about to undertake a military campaign. Having heard of Master Ling-shu's power to foresee the future, King Liu went to ask for his advice.

Master Ling-shu already knew the King's intention and passed away before he arrived. King Liu was enraged and demanded, "What caused the Master to pass away so quickly?"

The attendant answered candidly, "The Master knew that you were coming, so he decided to pass away before you arrived. He left a box for you."

King Liu opened the box and found a slip of paper inside which read: "The eyes of humans and heavenly beings are encompassed by the head monk at the teaching hall." King Liu understood the underlying implication of the message. He canceled his plans for war and invited Master Yün-men to become the Abbot of Ling-shu Temple.

The ancients seldom allowed an unqualified person to fill a position, preferring to leave it vacant until the right person came along. Although a person might have the necessary qualifications and virtue, he or she must wait for the right conditions to arise.

Master Ling-shu Ju-min waited twenty years for the right head monk. Hence, we can see how careful he was in choosing the right person for such an important position.

Begging to Help Others

While Ch'an Master Chao-yin was traveling one day, someone approached him and asked, "What should I do about my bad temper?"

The Master answered, "Bad temper arises from anger. I humbly beg you to give me your bad temper and anger."

Another time, Master Chao-yin discovered that one of his devotee's son was very lazy and liked to sleep. His parents did not know how to help him. When Master Chao-yin heard this, he went to his devotee's home, woke up the son, and said to him, "I came to ask for your lethargy. Give me your lethargy."

Yet, another instance, when Master Chao-yin heard that a couple, who were his devotees, were quarreling, the Master went to beg for their querulousness. Similarly, when a devotee abused alcohol, Master Chao-yin went to ask for the devotee's alcoholism.

Throughout his life, Master Chao-yin helped many people to overcome their bad habits by begging to assume their weaknesses.

A Pair of Pure Hands

Prime Minister P'ei-hsiu of the T'ang dynasty was a Ch'an practitioner. He recorded his insights which were derived from meditational practice and presented the account to Ch'an Master Huang-po.

The Master put the account on the desk without looking at it. After a long time, he asked P'ei-hsiu, "Do you understand my meaning?"

P'ei-hsiu answered frankly, "No, I don't."

Master Huang-po said, "The teaching of Ch'an is not dependent on the written word. By writing it down, you have actually destroyed the true meaning of Buddhism which is opposed to the teaching of Ch'an. Therefore, I refuse to look at it."

His words gave P'ei-hsiu a deeper understanding of Ch'an, and P'ei-hsiu's respect for Master Huang-po grew. He composed a verse in praise of the Master:

Since the Master inherited the mind-seal[14],
There is a pearl on the forehead of his seven
  foot body.
He stayed at Shu for ten years before coming
  to this side of River Chang.
Eight thousand disciples follow in his exalted
  steps;
Good causes gathered like fragrant flowers
  from afar.
I was going to be the Master's disciple,
Not knowing to whom the Master will reveal
  his teaching.

Master Huang-po neither praised nor condemned the verse but merely commented:

The mind is like a boundless sea;
Red lotuses that spit from the mouth can
  nurture the sick body.
A pair of pure hands will naturally develop
  that never yield to any ordinary person.

When Master Huang-po was sixty-five years old, P'ei-hsiu collected the Master's teachings in a volume, and later P'ei-hsiu collected a second volume. Master Huang-po read neither of them, demonstrating that he was true to the Ch'an teaching of avoiding dependence on written language.

How Can You Understand?

After Ch'an Master Yün-men attained realization under the instruction of Ch'an Master Mu-chou, he began to travel.

While in Kiangchou, Master Yün-men met an official named Chen-ts'ao, who also practiced Ch'an.

Chen-ts'ao questioned Yün-men, "What is the duty of a traveling monk?"

Yün-men replied indirectly, asking, "How many people have you asked this same question before you asked me?"

The official said, "Don't be concerned about the number of people whom I have asked. At the moment, I am asking you."

Yün-men inquired, "We shall discuss this later. Let me first ask you, what are the teachings of the *Tathāgata*?"

The official answered, "The yellow scrolls."

Yün-men reasoned, "They are only ink on paper and are not the essence of the Buddha's teaching. Try again. What is the teaching?"

The official replied, "It is at the tip of my tongue, but at the moment, I am at a loss for words. My mind wants to rationalize, but my thinking is gone."

Yün-men said, "Wanting to say it but finding oneself at a loss for words involves language. The mind that wants to reason, but finding oneself at a loss for thought involves illusory thinking. You have not said it right yet. Try again. What is the teaching?"

The official could not arrive at a response.

Yün-men queried, "I heard that you are studying the *Lotus Sutra*?"

The official made an affirmation by saying, "Yes."

Yün-men continued, "According to the *Lotus Sutra*: 'All livelihood and properties are in accordance with the true phenomena.' Please tell me how many people retire in the heaven where there is neither thinking nor not thinking?"

The official was again at a loss for words.

Yün-men remarked, "Reading the ten sutras and the five *śāstras* and then practicing in monasteries for ten or twenty years do not guarantee that one will attain enlightenment. What makes you think that you can understand the Buddha's teaching by reading only a few sutras?"

The official said, "Please forgive me."

After this encounter, Master Yün-men was invited to stay at the official's residence for three years.

Ch'an practitioners do not flaunt their attainments by boasting. When Yün-men first went to Mu-chou, he was hit three times and was ousted from the temple three times. He finally attained realization after much hard work. Thus, the official's reading of a few sutras was nothing compared to what Yün-men had undergone.

The Wonder of Chewing and Pecking

Ch'an Master Nan-yüan Hui-yung was a disciple of Ch'an Master Lin-chi.

Once, Hui-yung lectured his students by saying, "Most people today only know about the theory of chewing and pecking[15] simultaneously, but they have not experienced the wonder of such a practice."

Then a novice went forward and asked, "What is it like to be chewing and pecking simultaneously?"

Master Hui-yung explained, "Chewing and pecking are like striking stones to get a spark. It happens, instantaneously, without any hesitation, delay, or deliberation."

The novice was not satisfied and said, "I still have my doubts."

Master Hui-yung asked kindly, "What doubts do you have?"

The novice said scornfully, "I did not have any doubts before, but what you have just said now confuses me."

Master Hui-yung hit the novice with his staff and ousted him from the temple before he had a chance to explain himself.

This novice went to study with Master Yün-men and told a disciple of Master Yün-men how he was driven out by Master Hui-yung.

The disciple inquired, "When Master Hui-yung hit you, did his staff break?"

Upon hearing this, the novice attained realization and decided to return to Hui-yung to ask for his pardon. Unfortunately, Master Hui-yung had already passed away, and Master Fêng-hsüeh Yen-chao was the Abbot.

Master Yen-chao asked the novice, "What made you disagree with the Master?"

The novice replied, "I felt as if I were walking with a flickering light."

Master Yen-chao said, "Well, now that you understand, I will confirm your realization. "

According to a Chinese saying: "If the rice is not cooked, do not remove the lid. If the egg is not ready to be hatched, do not break it open."

The wonder of chewing and pecking is that it has to occur spontaneously, at the optimum moment, so a new life will be born.

When Master Hui-yung hit the novice and ousted him from the temple, the latter was still in a period of incubation. The disciple of Master Yün-men had pecked at the shell at just the right moment when he posed the question "Did the staff break?"

No Other Choice but to Speak

One day, Ch'an Master Tao-fu went to visit Ch'an Master Hsüeh-fêng I-ts'un. At their first meeting, Master Hsüeh-fêng asked, "Where do you live?"

Tao-fu replied, "Wenchou."

Master Hsüeh-fêng said, "Then you came from the same place as Ch'an Master Hsüan-chüeh Yung-chia."

Tao-fu was unsure and asked, "Where did Master Yung-chia live?"

Master Hsüeh-fêng scolded him, "You are so ignorant. I should give you a good beating, but I will let you off today."

"*Tang-tang-mi-mi-ti* (the ultimate truth manifests itself clearly at all places)" were the words spoken by Master Hsüeh-fêng as he addressed the assembly one day. After having said this, Master Hsüeh-fêng fell silent, and no one understood what he meant.

Tao-fu came forward and asked, "What is '*Tang-tang-mi-mi-ti*'?"

Master Hsüeh-fêng inquired, "What did you say?"

Tao-fu stood respectfully at attention.

Master Hsüeh-fêng waited, but no one spoke, so he continued, "'*Tang-tang-mi-mi-ti*' is the essence of the teaching of Ch'an."

Upon hearing this, Tao-fu knelt down, joined his palms together, and said, "I have been here for several years already and have never heard the Master offer such compassionate teachings."

Master Hsüeh-fêng said, "I have never spoken in this manner before. Does it bother you now that I have said it?"

Tao-fu remarked, "How dare I be bothered? There is nothing else you can do."

Master Hsüeh-fêng said, "You gave me no other choice but to speak."

From that time on, Tao-fu became a full-fledged Ch'an practitioner under Hsüeh-fêng's guidance.

Where Is the Highly Cultivated Monk?

Once, when Prime Minister P'ei-hsiu was visiting Lung-hsing Temple, he saw a painting and asked, "What kind of painting is this?"

The temple monk answered, "The true demeanor of a highly cultivated monk."

P'ei-hsiu questioned, "I can see the true demeanor, but where is the highly cultivated monk?'

The temple monk could not respond.

P'ei-hsiu asked, "Are there any Ch'an practitioners here?"

The temple monk answered, "We do have a roving monk who came here recently. He seems to be a Ch'an practitioner."

P'ei-hsiu asked to meet with this roving monk and said to him, "I had just asked the temple monk a question. I wonder whether you can answer it?"

The roving monk replied, "Please ask your question."

As P'ei-hsiu started to speak, the roving monk shouted, "Prime Minister!"

Naturally, P'ei-hsiu responded to his title.

"Where?" the roving monk asked.

P'ei-hsiu exclaimed, "So, you are the highly cultivated monk!"

P'ei-hsiu prostrated himself before the monk and asked to become his student. The roving monk was the famous Ch'an Master Huang-po.

Prime Minister P'ei-hsiu was a true follower of Master Huang-po's teaching—"Don't seek anything from the Buddha. Don't seek anything from the Dharma. Don't seek anything from the *Sangha*. This is the true way of practice."

No Buddha in the Buddha Hall

Ch'an Master Wu-yeh was tall and robust, with a voice resonant like a bell. When he first visited Ch'an Master Ma-tsu, Ma-tsu teased him, "What a magnificent Buddha hall, but there is no Buddha inside!"

Wu-yeh prostrated and respectfully replied, "I am confident that I know a brief account of the teaching of the three *yānas*. But I really don't understand the Ch'an teaching that 'the mind is the Buddha.'"

Since Wu-yeh was sincere, Ma-tsu said, "The mind that doesn't understand is it. There is nothing to it. When you don't understand, that is confusion. When you understand, that is realization. When you are confused, you are a sentient being. When you have achieved realization, you are the Buddha."

Wu-yeh asked, "Other than the mind, the Buddha, and sentient beings, is there any other Dharma?"

Ma-tsu commented, "The mind, the Buddha, and sentient beings are not different. How could there be any other Dharma?"

Wu-yeh inquired, "What was the meaning of the Patriarch's coming from the West?"[16]

Ma-tsu countered, "Where is the Patriarch now? Leave now and come back another time!" Master Wu-yeh took his leave and departed.

Suddenly, Ma-tsu hollered, "Venerable!"

Wu-yeh turned his head.

Ma-tsu said, "What is it?"

Master Wu-yeh knelt down, prostrated himself, and cried, "People say that the Buddha's Path is very long. I just realized today that the true form of the Dharma-body is originally present within us."

Ma-tsu said, "This dull fellow has finally reached realization!"

In terms of cultivation, what is the time interval needed to journey to the end of the Buddha's Path? If we say it entails a long time, then it can take as long as three great *kalpas*. If we say the time span is short, realization can be attained instantaneously. Because we have lost ourselves and tried to seek the Dharma externally, we need the Buddhas and patriarchs to teach us thousands of times before we can be convinced that we should turn our lives around.

After just one shout, Wu-yeh turned his head and immediately recognized his true face. According to a Chinese saying: "Don't seek water when you are a fish in the water. Don't look for the mountain when you are walking on it."

An Overturned Boat

A novice went to visit Ch'an Master Hsüeh-fêng, and the Master asked, "From where did you come?"

The novice answered, "I came from Ch'an Master Fu-ch'uan (literally, 'an overturned boat')."

Deliberately teasing him, Master Hsüeh-fêng remarked, "You have not crossed over the sea of life and death yet. Why did you overturn your boat?"

The novice did not understand what Master Hsüeh-fêng meant. When he returned to Master Fu-ch'uan, he told him what had happened.

Master Fu-ch'uan then said to the novice, "You are very foolish. Why didn't you say that you had already transcended the sea of life and death and that was why you overturned the boat?"

The novice went back to Master Hsüeh-fêng who inquired, "Since you have already overturned your boat, why did you come back?"

The novice replied confidently, "Since the cycle of life and death has already been transcended, why shouldn't I overturn the boat?"

Hsüeh-fêng said sternly, "This is not your own understanding. Your teacher taught you to say this. Take these twenty strokes back to your teacher, Fu-ch'uan, and tell him that I have also given myself twenty strokes. All these strokes had nothing to do with you."

Master Hsüeh-fêng gave Master Fu-ch'uan twenty strokes and gave himself twenty strokes. The underlying message is very clear: Ch'an should be free from the confines of language. Hsüeh-fêng and Fu-ch'uan were both playing language games, so each deserved twenty strokes. This had nothing to do with the novice, who was not yet worth twenty strokes.

Forgetting the Words

One day, Master Tung-shan observed a monk, who addressed an assembly without basing his lecture on any scriptures. The monk said to himself, "Wonderful! The Buddha and the Path are so incredible!"

Tung-shan went up to him and said, "I am not going to ask about the Buddha or the Path. I am interested in knowing the person who was talking about the Buddha and the Path just now?"

The monk was actually the head monk of the temple and was known as Head Monk Ch'u.

After listening to Tung-shan's words, Head Monk Ch'u remained silent.

However, Master Tung-shan would not let him go and persisted, "Why don't you speak up quickly?"

Head Monk Ch'u replied, "Nothing can be gained if I spoke."

Tung-shan was not satisfied, "You didn't even say anything. What do you mean by 'Nothing can be gained if I spoke'?"

After hearing this, the Head Monk again fell silent.

Master Tung-shan saw that he had made himself an enemy and said gently, "The Buddha and the Path are only empty names. Why don't you base your teachings on the doctrines?"

Head Monk Ch'u seized this opportunity and asked, "How is the doctrine being taught?"

Master Tung-shan clapped his hands, laughed, and exclaimed, "Forget the words when you realize the meaning!"

Sometimes, when Ch'an masters talk amongst themselves, they do not seem to make any sense. However, there is a lot of truth in what they say.

When Master Tung-shan urged Head Monk Ch'u to speak up immediately, the latter remained silent. When the Head Monk asked Tung-shan how to teach the doctrine, Tung-shan replied by saying, "Forget the words when you realize the meaning!"

Forgetting the words is the true practice of Ch'an.

Neither Questions nor Answers

A Ch'an master posed a riddle for his disciples to solve: "Two people are walking in a drizzle. Why does the sky not rain on one person?"

One disciple said, "One of them must be wearing a raincoat."

Another disciple attempted by saying, "It must have been a partial shower. One person gets rained on, whereas the other does not."

A third concluded, "The other person must be walking under a roof."

The Master finally explained, "All of you are clinging to the point that one person is not getting rained on and are fixated on that point. Thus, you are getting further and further away from the truth. When I asked, 'Why does the sky not rain on one person?' it implies that both people are being rained on!"

When we enter into a discussion on Ch'an, we should not approach it from the perspective of the question posed, but as in the above vignette, we should approach it from the standpoint of not asking any question.

There are thousands of Ch'an records, which make Ch'an look as if it were a teaching based on questions and answers. Sometimes, the questions do not really need to be answered. At other times, the answer does not pertain to what had been asked.

When there are questions and answers, arguments naturally arise. When one attains self-realization, there will be no arguments. The use of questions and answers should not be considered a guessing game. Other than the answer, what is there to be gained?

Not Emptying One's Cup

A scholar went to visit Ch'an Master Nan-yin and asked him to define Ch'an.

The Master poured a cup of tea for the scholar but continued to pour even though the tea was overflowing.

Having seen this, the scholar remarked, "Master, the cup is full."

But Master Nan-yin explained, "You are just like this cup, full of concepts and ideas. If you don't empty the cup that is in your mind first, then how can I begin to explain Ch'an to you?"

If people are arrogant and biased, even when heavenly nectar rains upon them, they will not benefit from it. Before we put the water

of truth into a container, it has to be emptied and cleansed first; otherwise, the taste of the water will be affected.

A Ch'an Master's Compassion

Ch'an Master Liang-k'uan had been practicing Ch'an diligently all his life. When he was old, he received news that his nephew did not have a proper job and had almost completely squandered the family's wealth. The family elders were very concerned and wanted Master Liang-k'uan to return and persuade his nephew to give up his bad habits. Out of compassion, Master Liang-k'uan decided to make the long journey home.

After three days of traveling, he finally reached his nephew's home, and his nephew was very happy to see him. Master Liang-k'uan stayed in his nephew's house that same evening.

The next morning, before Master Liang-kuan departed, he said to his nephew, "I think that I am really getting old. My hands are so shaky that I can't even tie my shoelaces. Could you help me?"

His nephew was more than happy to help.

Then Master Liang-k'uan said compassionately, "Thank you so much. You see, when a person gets old, he grows weaker and weaker by the day. So take care of yourself while you are still young. Be good and try to lay a firm foundation for your future."

After having said this, the Master turned around and left. He did not even mention a word about the nephew's misdeeds. But after the Master's visit, his nephew never misbehaved again.

The teaching of Ch'an varies. Sometimes, it consists of hitting and shouting or of questions and answers, while at other times it involves subtle discourse with underlying implications. No matter which method is used, a Ch'an master will never unravel the truth or the answer, because the truth or the answer belongs to us only when we have unraveled it for ourselves.

For parents who care about their children, do they understand this kind of Ch'an teaching?

Good and Evil Deeds

A monk asked Ch'an Master Chün-chi, "Who are the ones who do good?"

Chün-chi answered, "Those who wear shackles and chains."

The monk inquired again, "Who are the ones who do evil?"

Chün-chi replied, "Those who practice Ch'an and meditate."

The monk exclaimed, "I really have inferior roots! I cannot understand your point. Could you please explain it in simpler terms?"

Then Chün-chi said, "Those who are evil do not do good. Those who are good do not do evil." The monk was still confused.

After a while, Master Chün-chi asked him, "Do you understand now?"

The monk answered, "No."

Chün-chi commented, "Those who do evil have no good intentions. Those who do good have no evil intentions. We say good and evil are like floating clouds. There is neither arising nor destruction."

Finally, the monk understood.

From the conventional point of view, it is true that good begets good and evil begets evil. But from the perspective of self-nature, there are no such terms as good and evil. If we do not think in terms of good and evil, then the true self-nature can be seen.

The Master was not mistaken when he said that those who do good are the ones who wear shackles and chains, whereas those who do evil are the ones who practice Ch'an and meditate. Those who do good cling on to merits, which are no different from shackles and chains. Although those who do evil may fall into the realm of suffering, their true nature will not be altered in any way.

Master Chün-chi does not want us to be confused by the terms of good and evil. We need to understand that good and evil are dharmas, but the Dharma, itself, is neither good nor evil.

Who Is Our Posterity?

Ch'an Master T'ien-huang asked Ch'an Master Shih-t'ou, "Other than liberation, meditation, and wisdom, what else do you teach?"

Shih-t'ou said, "No one is in bondage. Why then should we talk about liberation?"

T'ien-huang inquired, "If you talk this way, how do you expect others to understand you?"

Shih-t'ou queried, "Do you know what 'emptiness'[17] is?"

"I had gained an understanding of 'emptiness' a long time ago."

Shih-t'ou remarked, "Ah! You are also from the delusory world."

T'ien-huang disagreed, "I am not from the delusory world."

Shih-t'ou continued, "I have known for a long time from where you came."

"How can you arrive at such conclusion without any evidence?"

Shih-t'ou replied, "Your body is evidence."

T'ien-huang retorted, "The four great elements are originally empty, and the five aggregates are non-existent, so what can we use to inspire and guide our posterity?"

Shih-t'ou shouted, "Tell me, who is our posterity?"

Finally, T'ien-huang understood.

The truth is that everything is empty; there is neither good nor evil. All dualistic concepts, such as bondage and liberation, emptiness and existence, in front and behind, are inconsistent with Ch'an. If practitioners can eliminate such concepts, they can certainly attain realization.

What Is Your Complaint?

Ch'an Master Chü-tun of Lung-ya Shan went to Chung-nan Shan to meditate under the guidance of Ch'an Master Ts'ui-wei. After several months, Master Ts'ui-wei still had not given him any instruction.

One day, he plucked up his courage and asked Master Ts'ui-wei,

"Ever since I came here, I have been meditating with the others, but I have not received any teaching from you. Why not?"

Master Ts'ui-wei inquired, "What is your complaint?"

Because Chü-tun had not gained the essence of the teaching, he left Master Ts'ui-wei and went to Tê-shan hoping to learn from Ch'an Master Hsüan-chien.

Once, he said to Master Hsüan-chien, "I have always admired your teaching. I have been here for quite a while, and yet I have never heard the teaching of the Master."

Master Hsüan-chien seemed to have been in communication with Master Ts'ui-wei, because he said, "What is your complaint?"

Disappointed, Chü-tun went to study with Master Tung-shan Liang-chieh.

One day, Chü-tun asked, "I beg you, please tell me one word about the essence of the Buddha's teaching."

Master Tung-shan said straightforwardly, "I will tell you when the water in the cave flows against the current."

When he heard this, Chü-tun attained realization.

To meditate with doubt, to meditate with intuition, or to meditate with a skeptical spirit—these are not as good as using one's everyday mind to meditate.

We are all living in delusion and are drifting with the currents of birth and death. If we can gain an understanding of the meaning of the cave water flowing against the current, then our true nature will be revealed.

What Is the Buddha Mind?

Ch'an Master Hui-chung once asked Master Tzŭ-lin, "You have been studying Buddhism for many years. What is the meaning of 'Buddha'?"

Without thinking, Tzŭ-lin answered, "Buddha means the 'Enlightened One.'"

Master Hui-chung inquired, "Will the Buddha become deluded?"

Becoming impatient, Tzŭ-lin challenged him, "If he is already the Buddha, then how can he possibly become deluded?"

Hui-chung countered, "If he is not deluded, what is the use of enlightenment?"

Tzŭ-lin had nothing to say in reply.

While Tzŭ-lin was writing a commentary for a sutra, Master Hui-chung said to him, "A person who writes a commentary should be in harmony with the Buddha-mind. One should attain a true understanding of the Buddha's teaching and know very clearly the needs of all beings; only then will one be able to write well."

Tzŭ-lin was displeased with these remarks and declared, "You are right. That is precisely why I started to write the commentary."

Upon hearing this, Master Hui-chung had someone bring a bowl of water containing seven grains of rice and a pair of chopsticks, and he asked Tzŭ-lin what they meant.

Again, Tzŭ-lin could not answer.

Master Hui-chung reprimanded him by saying, "You can't even understand my meaning. How can you claim that you are in harmony with the Buddha-mind?"

The bowl of water, the grains of rice, and the pair of chopsticks imply that Buddhism is not isolated from everyday life. What good is Buddhism if it is divorced from life? Master Tzŭ-lin had been writing commentaries that were irrelevant to everyday life. Therefore, he had already been estranged from the Buddha-mind.

The Sixth Patriarch, Hui-nêng, observed: "The Dharma is right here in this world; it is to be realized without departing from this world. If we leave this world and try to seek *bodhi*, then it would be like seeking the horns of a rabbit." A true Ch'an practitioner does not practice Ch'an as if it were something separate from this world or outside of ordinary life.

A Bundle of Firewood

Once, Ch'an Master Shih-t'ou of Nan-yüeh, Hunan, asked a student monk, "From where did you come?"

The student answered, "From Kiangsi."

Then Shih-t'ou continued, "Did you see Ch'an Master Ma-tsu?"

The student said, "Yes."

After learning this, Shih-t'ou pointed to a bundle of firewood and asked, "Does Master Ma-tsu resemble that bundle of firewood?"

The student did not know how to respond. Since he did not understand the teaching of Master Shih-t'ou, the student returned to Master Ma-tsu and reported what had happened. After listening to the student, Master Ma-tsu smiled and asked him, "How heavy was that bundle of firewood?"

The student said, "I did not weigh it."

Then, Ma-tsu remarked, "You must be very strong."

Baffled, the student asked, "Why?"

Ma-tsu answered, "You have carried that bundle of firewood all the way from Nan-yüeh to here. Doesn't that demonstrate your strength?"

This student monk wandered from place to place making negative remarks about various Ch'an masters behind their backs. Instead of becoming upset, Ma-tsu taught the novice a lesson.

Today, we also see many Buddhist followers going from one teacher to another, carrying with them bundles of firewood. One wonders whether they find the bundles heavy or not.

The *Mani* Pearl

When the Buddha was on Vulture Peak[18], he showed a *mani* pearl[19] to the four Celestial Kings[20] and asked, "What color is this *mani* pearl?"

In response, each used different colors to describe it.

The Buddha put away the pearl and asked again, "Now what is the color of the *mani* pearl in my hand?"

The four Celestial Kings did not understand what the Buddha meant and replied, "Buddha, there is nothing in your hand."

The Buddha then said, "I showed you an ordinary pearl, and you could all tell me its color. Now I am showing you a real pearl, and yet you can't see it! How confused you are!"

The real *mani* pearl is the true mind that is within each and every person. Worldly people are entrenched in seeking wealth and glory, but little do they realize that all worldly treasures are delusive. If we would all seek the treasure that is within every one of us with the same effort and energy we expend on worldly endeavors, we would find unlimited riches.

Letters from a Mother

When Ch'an Master Hui-hsin was a novice monk of fifteen, he was very clever. Because of this, he was granted an audience with the emperor and was given many gifts. To demonstrate his filial piety, he sent the emperor's gifts to his mother.

After receiving the gifts, his mother wrote him a letter, stating: "I was very happy with the gifts that you sent me, particularly because they were given to you by the emperor. However, when I had sent you to the monastery, I wanted you to become a true Ch'an practitioner and not someone who becomes lost in wealth and glory. If you are only busying yourself with vanities, then you are going against my wishes. I hope that you will remember the duty of a true Ch'an practitioner."

After receiving this letter from his mother, Hui-hsin decided to become a true Ch'an practitioner and not concern himself with the pursuit of fame and fortune.

Another time, Hui-hsin wanted to go home to visit his mother. Again, his mother wrote to him: "I have already sent you to the monastery. You now belong to the monastery and to all beings. You are no longer my private possession. From now on, you are the 'son of the Buddha.' You should respect your teachers and the Three Precious Ones and should not think of your mother anymore."

After receiving these two letters from his mother, Hui-hsin decided to devote all his time and effort to learning the Dharma, which enabled him to become a true Ch'an practitioner.

Selling Raw Ginger

Ch'an Master Pao-shou was the keeper of the storehouse at Wu-tsu Temple. At that time, Chieh-kung was the abbot. Occasionally, when Chieh-kung was sick and needed some raw ginger for his medicine, his attendant would go to the storehouse to get some. Instead of giving the attendant the ginger, Pao-shou would scold him and send him away.

When Chieh-kung heard about this, he gave the attendant some money and told him to buy some ginger from Pao-shou. Only then would Pao-shou give the attendant some ginger.

Later, when Tung-shan Temple needed an abbot, the county official wrote and asked Chieh-kung to recommend someone. Chieh-kung suggested, "That fellow who sold the raw ginger can be the Abbot of Tung-shan Temple."

Hence, Pao-shou became the Abbot of Tung-shan Temple, and the story entitled "The Raw Ginger of Pao-shou Is Hot for Ten Thousand Years" became very famous among Ch'an adepts.

Pao-shou was faithful to his office and refused to abuse his authority. Appreciating Pao-shou's loyalty, Chieh-kung suggested him to become the new abbot of Tung-shan Temple. Both are fitting examples to follow.

Where Are You Going to Squat?

A novice monk asked Ch'an Master Hsi-shan, "What was the meaning of the Patriarch's coming from the West?"

Master Hsi-shan held up a whisk in response. The novice monk was not satisfied with this answer, so he left and went to Ch'an Master Hsüeh-fêng instead.

Hsüeh-fêng asked, "From where did you come?"

The novice answered, "This summer, I came from Master Su-chou Hsi-shan."

Hsüeh-fêng then asked, "How is Master Hsi-shan?"

"When I left, everything was fine," replied the novice.

Hsüeh-fêng continued, "Why didn't you stay and learn from him?"

"He does not understand the Patriarchs' Ch'an," the novice replied.

Hsüeh-fêng asked, "What makes you think so?"

"When I asked him, 'What was the meaning of the Patriarch's coming from the West?' he held up his whisk and did not respond to my question."

Hsüeh-fêng continued the conversation by asking, "Have you seen the men and women of Suchou?"

"Yes!" exclaimed the novice.

"Did you see any flowers and trees on your way?"

Again, the novice exclaimed, "Yes!"

Then Hsüeh-fêng said, "All right. When you see men and women, you know they are obviously different. When you see flowers and trees, you are aware that they have various names and have unique functions. The rivers, mountains, and the great earth did not speak to you about the Dharma, yet you comprehended their meaning, correct?"

The novice agreed.

Hsüeh-fêng queried, "When Master Hsi-shan held up his whisk in reply to your question, why didn't you understand the Dharma that was implicit in it?"

After hearing this, the novice suddenly understood the underlying implication. He thanked Master Hsüeh-fêng and said, "I was careless in what I said. I beg your pardon! I would like to return to Ch'an Master Hsi-shan to ask for his forgiveness."

Hsüeh-fêng replied, "The whole universe is an eye. Where are you going to squat?"

Although the novice could not find a place to squat, he embraced the universe within himself. Although his physical eyes did not recognize the Master's whisk, he possessed the eye of wisdom which enabled him to see the entire universe. As one repents [liberates oneself from past attachments and illusions], one's mind is awakened in one instant of thought. The entire universe and great earth are recognized as the Dharma. This is what is meant by saying that raising the whisk can bring forth awakening.

Real Lies and False Lies?

Once, Ch'an Master Tao-kuang asked Ch'an Master Ta-chu Hui-hai, "Master, how do you use the mind to practice the Path?"

"I have no mind to use and no path to practice." Ta-chu replied.

After having pondered on this response, Tao-kuang asked, "If you have no mind to use and no path to practice, then why do you gather followers and encourage them to meditate and practice the Path?"

"I neither have a roof above me, nor do I have a space where I could stand. Where would I find a place to gather followers?"

Tao-kuang said, "But it is true that you gather followers every day to talk about the Path. Is this not teaching the Dharma?"

Ta-chu countered, "Please, don't make such false accusations about me. I can't even speak. How can I talk about the Dharma? I don't see even a single person. How can you say that I am gathering followers?"

Accusingly, Tao-kuang said, "Master, you are lying."

Ta-chu remarked, "I don't even have a tongue. How can I lie?"

Tao-kuang inquired, "Are you trying to tell me that this world, including all the beings, your existence and mine, meditation and the teaching of the Dharma, are all unreal?"

Ta-chu exclaimed, "They are real!"

Tao-kuang queried, "If they are all real, then why do you deny them?"

Ta-chu declared, "We have to deny the false as well as the real!"

Tao-kuang became enlightened at that instant.

Sometimes we have to understand the truth by affirmation, and at other times, we have to see it by negation. According to the *Heart Sutra*, "Form is emptiness, emptiness is form. This is also true for feeling, perception, volition, and consciousness ..." This means that we can understand life and the phenomenal world through affirmation. The *Heart Sutra* also states: "No eyes, ears, nose, tongue, body, or mind; no form, sound, smell, taste, touch, or idea..." This statement implies that we can understand life and the phenomenal world by negation. When Master Ta-chu Hui-hai denied everything, he was not lying because negating everything would actually be the same as affirming everything.

Mind and Nature

A novice monk went to Ch'an Master Nan-yang Hui-chung and asked, "Ch'an is another name for mind. 'Mind' is the true nature that is neither more in the Buddha nor less in the average person. The Ch'an patriarchs change the name of this 'mind' into 'nature.' May I ask, Master, what is the difference between mind and nature?"

Hui-chung answered, "There is a difference when one is deluded. However, if one is enlightened, there is no difference."

The novice further asked, "The sutra states that the Buddha-nature is permanent whereas the mind is impermanent; why do you say that there is no difference?"

Master Hui-chung patiently replied, "You only understand this by the characters and not by its implication. For instance, when the temperature drops to the freezing point, water will freeze into ice, and when the temperature rises, ice will melt into water. Similarly, when one is deluded, one's self-nature will turn into the mind, and the mind will turn into self-nature when one becomes enlightened. The mind and self-nature are originally the same. The distinction depends on whether one is deluded or enlightened." Finally, the novice understood.

In Buddhist terminology, mind and self-nature have many synonyms such as "true face," "*tathāgatagarbha* (the womb or the storehouse of Buddha's teaching)," "*dharmakāya* (the absolute or spiritual body)," "absolute reality," "*bhūtatathatā* (suchness or thusness)," "the true body," "true mind," "*prajñā*," "Ch'an," and so on. The purpose of all these synonyms is to help us understand ourselves. While some people are more deluded than others, the true nature of each individual does not differ. It is just like gold, which can be made into different shapes of varying sizes, such as earrings, bracelets, necklaces, and so on, but the nature of the gold does not change. Similarly, mind and nature may constitute different names, but both are actually our essence.

The Nature of Worldly Virtues

Ch'an Master Yün-chü built a hut at Ch'an Master Tung-shan Liang-chieh's temple and went on a solitary retreat.

Once, Master Yün-chü had not gone to the dining hall for ten consecutive days. Hence, Master Tung-shan was concerned and also wondered what Yün-chü was doing. As a result, he sent for Master Yün-chü and asked him, "Why haven't you come to eat recently?"

Master Yün-chü said elatedly, "A *deva* brings me food every day!"

Upon hearing this, Tung-shan said scornfully, "I had suspected that you were only an uncultivated person who clings to worldly virtues! I'll see you tomorrow!"

The next day, Yün-chü went to see Master Tung-shan. Tung-shan loudly shouted his name. Yün-chü replied politely. Tung-shan suddenly asked, "Which is better, worldly virtues or realizing the nature of worldly virtues?"

Yün-chü was dumbfounded. Consumed with doubts, he returned to his hut. In solitude, he began to contemplate. For three days, the *deva* did not bring him any food. Finally, he realized the unconditioned state in which he could enjoy the nourishing power of Ch'an.

Worldly virtues are not something that Ch'an practitioners should cling to, because worldly virtues are as impermanent as any other worldly phenomenon. Instead, a Ch'an practitioner should cultivate the Ch'an mind, transcending worldly honor and dishonor, right and wrong.

Nothing Is Attainable

One day, Ch'an Master Yang-shan Hui-chi asked Ch'an Master Shuang-fêng, "Dharma brother, what type of understanding have you attained from your practice?"

"According to what I know, nothing is attainable."

Hui-chi said, "Now, you are remaining in a worldly state."

Shuang-fêng questioned, "I have already attained the state where nothing is attainable. How, then, can you say that I am remaining in a worldly state?"

Hui-chi retorted, "You think that you have attained the state where nothing is attainable, but in fact, that is attaining something."

Shuang-fêng remarked, "This is the best I can do. I am no longer attracted by sensual pleasure, nor is my mind disturbed by what is going on around me. Dharma brother, what do you think I should do?"

Hui-chi asked, "Why don't you go and seek after the truth that is implicit in 'nothing is attainable'?"

When their teacher, Ch'an Master Kuei-shan Ling-yu, heard this, he was pleased and said, "Hui-chi, what you have just said will cause great doubt in the minds of all those under heaven."

Shuang-fêng still did not understand and thought: "Since nothing is attainable, what is there to seek after?"

Master Ling-yu knew what Shuang-fêng was thinking, so he said to him, "You are one of those under heaven."

A Ch'an practitioner should practice and gain the understanding of "no practice" and should attain the state of "no attainment" because the practice of "no practice" is "true practice," and the attainment of "no attainment" is "true attainment."

Can You Hear?

Prime Minister Tu Hung-chien was discussing the Dharma with Ch'an Master Wu-chu at the back of the monastery, while a crow was crowing on a tree. Master Wu-chu asked the Prime Minister whether he heard the crow crowing. The Prime Minister answered, "Yes, I can hear it."

The crow then flew away, and Master Wu-chu asked the Prime Minister whether he still heard the crow crowing. The Prime Minister answered, "No, I don't hear it any more."

Master Wu-chu declared, "I can still hear the crow crowing."

The Prime Minister asked suspiciously, "But the crow has already flown away. Why do you say that you still can hear it crowing?"

Master Wu-chu explained, "Whether one hears it or not has

nothing to do with the nature of hearing, which is neither produced nor can it be destroyed. When there is sound, the quality of the sound arises of its own accord. When there is no sound, the quality of sound ceases of its own accord. Hearing does not arise or cease when the sound arises and ceases. If we understand the nature of hearing from this perspective, then we shall never be affected by sound. We should recognize that sound is impermanent and that hearing neither arises nor ceases. While the crow can come and go, our hearing does not come or go."

Finally, the Prime Minister understood.

All phenomena in this world are relative; for example, we have coming and going, up and down, having and not having, arising and ceasing, and so on. Due to our delusions, we make all sorts of distinctions and experience many kinds of attachment. If we truly understand that the crowing of the crow comes and goes and cannot be moved by worldly phenomena, then we will sincerely appreciate the beautiful sound of "one hand clapping[21]."

The Worries of Buddha

A devotee asked Ch'an Master Chao-chou Tsung-shen, "Does the Buddha have worries?"

Chao-chou exclaimed, "Yes!"

The devotee queried, "Buddha is already enlightened, so why does he still have worries?"

Chao-chou answered, "That is because you are still not liberated from suffering."

The devotee inquired, "If I cultivate myself and become liberated from suffering, will the Buddha still have worries?"

Chao-chou again exclaimed, "Yes!"

Then the devotee questioned again, "If I am already liberated, why does the Buddha still have worries?"

Chao-chou declared, "Because many beings still exist!"

The devotee asked, "But it is not possible to liberate every being from suffering. Does this mean that the Buddha will always have worries and can never transcend them?"

Chao-chou answered, "The Buddha has already transcended and detached himself from worries."

The devotee questioned, "If all beings have not been freed yet, how can the Buddha no longer have any worries?"

Chao-chou replied, "Because within the self-nature of the Buddha all beings have already been freed."

At this point, the devotee seemed to have attained a further understanding.

The worries of average people and sentient beings arise from ignorance, whereas the worries of the Buddha arise due to his compassion. From the perspective of *prajñā*, the Buddha has no worries. Do our worries arise out of our compassion or through *prajñā*? We should beware to guard against the worries that arise from ignorance.

Skin Wrapped in Bones

A novice saw a turtle by the side of the temple and asked Ch'an Master Ta-sui, "The bones of most animals are wrapped by their skin. Why is it that the skin of the turtle is wrapped by its bones."

Instead of answering verbally, Master Ta-sui took off his straw sandal and covered the turtle with it.

Ch'an Master Shou-tuan wrote a verse about this incident:

> The skin of a turtle is obviously covered by a
>   layer of bone;
> Even the cracks and patterns are clearly seen.
> Covering it with the straw sandal,
> The novice could not understand Ta-sui's
>   meaning.

Ch'an Master Fo-têng also wrote a verse:

> The Dharma does not arise on its own,
> But arises from the right conditions.
> A turtle does not know how to climb a wall,
> A straw sandal is used by people for walking.

Ch'an Master Pao-fêng also clearly noted:

> A bell is made to be struck,
> The spokes of a wheel are made of iron.
> Water flows toward the east,
> While the sun goes down in the west!

People are curious about their surroundings. This curiosity encourages the pursuit of knowledge, but it is also a hindrance to the attainment of enlightenment. The everyday mind is the mind of enlightenment.

The novice was curious to know why the turtle's skin was covered by bone. Master Ta-sui covered up the turtle with his straw sandal to cover up the source of our delusion.

Master Fo-têng wrote: "A turtle does not know how to climb a wall, A straw sandal is used by people for walking." Master Pao-fêng wrote: "Water flows toward the east, While the sun goes down in the west!" Although these are common sense expressions, there is something extraordinary within this commonness, namely the law of conditioned co-production. If we understand this, then this would be the Dharma, this would be the mind of Ch'an, and this would be enlightenment!

To Beat and to Bellow

For a long time, Ch'an masters were known to be fond of carrying staffs with them as symbols of authority. These masters did not beat the students with their staffs very often, but rather, they were intended to convey a certain message while discussing Ch'an *kung-ans*.

Once, two Dharma brothers went to Ch'an Master Wu-tê for instruction. Every time they went in for instruction, the Master would beat them. The Master was so agile and accurate that the two could never escape his blows.

The two finally discussed the situation. The younger one said, "We have been here for quite a while, and so far we only get beatings and have attained no realization. I really want to leave, but to find someone better than Master Wu-tê is not easy."

The older one suggested, "How about this—the next time we go for instruction, we'll simply stand outside the hall. No matter how quick the Master is, he would not be able to hit us."

The next day, the two of them stood outside the hall and asked, "Please tell us the meaning of the Patriarch's coming from the West?"

Master Wu-tê bellowed, "You disrespectful creatures!"

The two were so startled by his shout that they both knelt down and said, "We never knew that the Master's bellowing is much faster and more powerful than his beatings."

A Ch'an practitioner should never seek "instant" realization. If we have not practiced on our own, it does not matter how much a master says, beats, or bellows at us, for we will never attain realization.

With solid practice, a simple word, a beating, or a bellow at the right moment will help us attain realization instantaneously.

You Are a Buddha

There were two brothers who practiced Ch'an together. The older brother observed the precepts[22] very strictly, while the younger brother was lackadaisical and liked to drink.

One day, the younger brother was drinking in his room when the older brother happened to pass by. The younger brother called out, "Brother, come and join me for a drink."

The older brother said scornfully, "You really have no shame. When are you going to quit?"

The younger brother shouted back, "You do not even know how to drink. You are not a man."

Angrily, the older brother countered, "Tell me, if I am not a man, what am I?"

The younger brother said, "You are a Buddha."

What a wonderful reply! Using the humor of a Ch'an master, one simple word can change war into peace.

Smashing the Bones of Emptiness

When Ch'an Master Meng-ch'uang was still a novice, he traveled for thousands of miles to the capital to study with Ch'an Master I-shan.

One day, he asked the Master, "I am still not clear about the Dharma, could you please instruct me?"

Master I-shan said sternly, "My teaching does not contain a single word or phrase, nor do I have any Dharma to impart."

Meng-ch'uang pleaded, "Would the Master please be compassionate and use your expedient means?"

Coldly, I-shan replied, "I have no expedient means, nor do I have any compassion."

After several attempts, Meng-ch'uang still did not understand I-shan's teaching. He thought: "Since the Master will not teach me anything, even if I stay here, I will not attain realization." Therefore, he left I-shan and went to Ch'an Master Fo-kuo.

At Master Fo-kuo's temple, he encountered ruthless beatings. This was too much for Meng-ch'uang. He left Master Fo-kuo, saying, "If I do not attain realization, I will never come back to see you again."

From then on, Meng-ch'uang spent his time meditating day and night. One day, while he was sitting underneath a tree, his mind was devoid of attachments. Late at night, Meng-ch'uang returned to his room to rest. When he got in bed, he mistakenly leaned against what he thought was the wall and fell. Immediately, he started to laugh. At that very instant, he became enlightened and expressed his feelings in the following verse:

> Many years spent digging in the dirt,
> Looking for the blue sky.
> Layers and layers of obstacles were found.

One night after hitting the wall in the dark,
The bones of emptiness were smashed into
  pieces.

To express his gratitude after enlightenment, he went to see Masters I-shan and Fo-kuo, presenting his realization to them.

Fo-kuo praised him and affirmed his realization by saying, "Now that you have understood the meaning of the Patriarch's coming from the West, you must take good care of yourself."

Ch'an masters, both in the past and in the present, share one characteristic. Most of them behave in a very intimidating manner, although their hearts are filled with compassion. When I-shan said that he had no expedient means and no compassion, he was actually showing his expedient means and demonstrating his compassion.

The beatings administered by Master Fo-kuo were the way he expressed his expedient means and compassion. If the Master had not utilized such a method, Meng-ch'uang would never have attained realization.

Spring wind and summer rain can nurture; however, autumn frost and winter snow are also necessary for the growth of all things. Accordingly, various expedient means are employed by Ch'an masters to guide people along the Path of spiritual maturity.

Seeking Nothing

Ch'an Master Hsüeh-tou of the Sung dynasty met a Confucian scholar by the name of Tseng-hui by the Huai River.

Tseng-hui asked, "Master, where are you going?"

Hsüeh-tou answered very politely, "I am not sure. Maybe I'll go to Ch'ien-t'ang or perhaps in the direction of T'ien-t'ai."

Tseng-hui suggested, "Ch'an Master Shan of Ling-yin Temple is a good friend of mine. I will write a letter of recommendation for you. I am sure that he will look after you."

When he arrived at Ling-yin Temple, Master Hsüeh-tou neither showed his letter of recommendation nor asked to see the abbot. He simply joined the other monks.

Three years later, Tseng-hui was transferred to Chekiang. One day, he went to Ling-yin Temple to visit Master Hsüeh-tou, but no one in the temple knew who Hsüeh-tou was. Tseng-hui could not believe it, so he went to the monks' quarter to see for himself. It took him a long time before he recognized Hsüeh-tou, who was amongst the one thousand monks staying at Ling-yin Temple. He asked Hsüeh-tou, "Why are you hiding here? Why didn't you go to see the abbot? Did you lose the recommendation letter that I gave you?"

Hsüeh-tou replied, "How dare I? I am only a cloud and water (roving) monk. I am seeking nothing, so I don't have any desire to be your messenger."

He took out the sealed letter and returned it to Tseng-hui, and they both laughed heartily. Tseng-hui introduced Hsüeh-tou to Abbot Shan, who greatly treasured Hsüeh-tou's talent. Later, when Ts'ui-fêng Temple of Suchou needed an abbot, Master Shan recommended Hsüeh-tou for the position.

Although Hsüeh-tou had the opportunity to assume a high position, he was patient enough to wait for the right moment. This is an ideal example that we should all follow. If we study assiduously and work diligently, then others will recognize our ability and give us our proper due. A Chinese proverb states: "Do not be concerned with your position, but rather, place your concerns on whether you have set your goals properly." This implies that if we set our goals properly and work diligently to reach them, we will eventually succeed.

Looking for the Antelope

Six novices went to study with Ch'an Master Huang-po. When they saw the Master, five of them respectfully prostrated themselves, while one pretended to be a Ch'an practitioner.

The imitator held up his sitting mat, and without uttering a word, he made a circle in the air with it. Then, he stood to one side.

Huang-po said to this monk, "I heard that there is a hunting dog that is very fierce."

The novice, answering in such a manner as if he was a Ch'an master, declared, "It must have heard the antelope."

Then Huang-po queried, "Did you hear the antelope?"

The novice replied, "It must have seen the antelope's footprint."

Huang-po continued, inquiring, "Did you see the antelope's footprint?"

The novice retorted, "It must have followed behind the antelope."

Huang-po asked, "Did you see the antelope?"

The novice answered, "It is dead."

Then Huang-po left.

The next day Huang-po mentioned this incident and said, "The novice who was looking for the antelope yesterday, please come forward."

After hearing this, the novice quickly went forward.

Huang-po remarked, "Our discussion on yesterday's *kung-an* is not quite finished yet. How are you going to explain it?"

The novice was unable to give a reply.

Huang-po said, "I was going to say that you are skilled at Ch'an. Now, I know that you only understand Ch'an intellectually."

As a result, the novice was ousted from the temple as an impostor.

Ch'an is the natural expression of our inner realization. It is not something that can be imitated. Knowledge can be learned, but Ch'an cannot be learned. Ch'an practitioners may seem to speak or behave strangely, but wisdom underlies their strangeness.

The Cloud in the Blue Sky

Li Ao, a government official of Langchou during the T'ang dynasty, greatly respected the virtues of Ch'an Master Yao-shan Wei-yen.

One day, Li Ao went to visit the Master. When he arrived, the Master was reading under a tree. Although the Master knew that Li Ao had come, he had no intention of getting up to greet him. When his attendant announced the arrival of Li Ao, Master Wei-yen ignored him and continued reading.

Li Ao was irritated and said testily, "What I see here is not as great as what I have heard." He turned around and prepared to leave.

Coldly, Master Wei-yen replied, "Why do you value what you hear and disdain what you see?"

Li Ao was moved by what the Master had just said. Turning around, he apologized and asked, "What is the Buddha's teaching?"

Master Wei-yen pointed upward, then downward, and asked, "Do you understand?"

Li Ao shook his head and said, "No."

Wei-yen said, "The cloud in the blue sky and the water in the jar."

Li Ao was pleased with this response. He bowed and recited the following verse:

> His physical body was like that of a crane,
> Reading sutras under thousands of pines;
> When I went to inquire about the Buddhist
>   teaching,
> He said, 'The cloud in the blue sky and the
>   water in the jar.'

Today, when people are being introduced to others for the first time, they often say, "I have heard about you for a long time." At the same time, they might be thinking to themselves, "There is really nothing special about this person." This implies "valuing the ears and disdaining the eyes," which is typical of human nature. Because Li Ao was a high-ranking official and a Confucian scholar, he was very arrogant. The coldness that Master Yao-shan displayed was humiliating to him, which simply depicted the difference between the state of mind of a Ch'an adept and that of a Confucian scholar.

Not Believing Is the Truth

A novice asked Ch'an Master Hui-chung, "The ancients said that the green bamboos are the true nature of the Buddha, and the blooming yellow flowers do not differ from *prajñā*. Those who do not believe this will be regarded as heretics. Those who believe in this will think that it is incredible. So, who is right?"

Master Hui-chung answered, "This is the state of mind of Mañjuśrī and Samantabhadra. An average mind cannot really comprehend this. The *Avatamsaka Sutra* states: 'The Buddha's body fills the whole universe, and he presents himself equally to all beings. He manifests himself in all forms and in all places according to the needs of all beings, and yet he never leaves his seat of *bodhi*!' The green bamboos do not exist outside of this universe. Thus, they have to be a part of the true nature of the Buddha. It also says in the *Prajñā Sutra* that forms are limitless, thus *prajñā* is also limitless. Since yellow flowers are forms, they do not differ from *prajñā*. Therefore, nothing is absolute."

After listening to this explanation, the novice still did not understand, and he further inquired, "In regards to this, is the believer correct or is the non-believer correct?"

Master Hui-chung, attempting to point to a higher state of mind, answered, "The believers belong to the level of conventional truth, whereas the skeptics belong to the level of the Ultimate Truth."[23]

The novice was surprised by these remarks and said, "But the skeptics criticize this as heresy. How can the Master say that they belong to the level of the Ultimate Truth?"

The Master stated, "Skeptics will not believe, and the Ultimate Truth will always remain ultimate. Because it is the Ultimate Truth, average people will criticize it as heresy. How can one talk about the Ultimate Truth with a heretic?"

Finally, the novice realized that it was not easy to believe in the Ultimate Truth.

When Śākyamuni Buddha was enlightened, he realized that his understanding was contrary to what others understood. All beings regard sensual pleasure as real, whereas the Buddha regards sensual pleasure as unreal. All beings regard the Buddha-nature as nonexistent, whereas the Buddha regards it as existent. Thus, we should not make judgments about truthfulness simply on the basis of someone's belief or disbelief or on someone's judgments of good or bad. Regardless of what others believe or say, the truth remains the truth.

The Wondrous Use of Ch'an

When Ch'an Master Hsien-yai was traveling on the road, he met a quarreling couple.

The wife yelled, "You are not a man!"

The husband shouted, "Say that one more time and I will hit you!"

The wife screeched, "So what? You are not a man!"

Listening to the couple quarreling, Master Hsien-yai started shouting, "Come, come and watch! You have to pay to watch a bullfight or cockfight, but you do not need to pay to watch people fight! Come and watch!"

The couple continued quarreling.

The husband threatened, "If you say that one more time, I will surely kill you!"

The wife exclaimed, "Go ahead and kill me! You are not a man!"

Hsien-yai declared, "Oh! It is becoming more and more exciting. They are going to kill each other. Come quickly and watch."

Then a spectator rebuked, "Hey, monk! What are you screaming about? Their quarreling is none of your business."

Hsien-yai said, "But it is my business. Didn't you hear that they are going to kill each other? If one of them is killed, there will be a need for someone to perform the funeral ceremony. I can make money if I am asked to perform the ceremony."

The spectator was appalled and exclaimed, "You are crazy in wanting others to kill just so that you can earn some money!"

Hsien-yai replied, "I can also stop them from killing each other, but in order to do that, I have to start teaching them the Dharma."

Instead of continuing with their quarrel, the couple began to listen to the argument between Hsien-yai and the spectator.

Hsien-yai started to counsel the couple, "Ice, no matter how thick it is, will melt when the sun comes out. A grain of rice, no matter how hard it is, will be soften when cooked over a fire. You are husband and wife because you have a special affinity towards each other. You should be the sun that warms each other, and you should be the fire that helps the other realize his or her potential. I hope that you will learn to live with each other and respect each other."

Master Hsien-yai demonstrated the wondrous use of Ch'an.

The Essence of Ch'an

Pai Chü-i, who was a famous poet, asked Ch'an Master Wei-k'uan, "How should our bodies, speech, and minds be used in our practice?"

Wei-k'uan said, "If we practice the supreme *bodhi* with our bodies, then we are observing the precepts. If we express it with our mouths, then that is the Dharma. If we practice it with our minds, then it is Ch'an. Although it can have three different functions, its purpose is the same. The River Huai and the River Han have different names, but the nature of their water is not different. The precepts are not different from the Dharma, and the Dharma is the same as Ch'an. If our bodies, speech, and minds can be exercised together, then the three of them are one in our hearts. Why should you draw any distinctions among them?"

Pai Chü-i questioned, "If there are no distinctions, why do we have to cultivate our minds?"

Wei-k'uan said, "If our minds are originally pure, why do they have to be cultivated? You should understand regardless of its purity or impurity. Not allowing any thought to arise is the most crucial point!"

Pai Chü-i reasoned, "Impurities are like dirt that can be wiped away. Thus, we should not give rise to such thoughts. With regard to purity, can we also not give rise to such thoughts?"

Wei-k'uan said, "For instance, our eyes cannot tolerate any substance that blocks them. Although gold dust is valuable, it will hurt our eyes if we try to put it in them. Dark clouds can cover the sky, so can white clouds."

Pai Chü-i said, "One who does not practice or has no thoughts is no different from an average person."

Wei-k'uan said, "An average person is always ignorant. Followers of the two *yānas* always cling to what they practice. If one can be freed from these two sicknesses of ignorance and clinging, then one will engage in true practice. A true practitioner is neither overly zealous nor overly forgetful. Zealousness is close to clinging, and forgetfulness is close to ignorance. This is the essence of Ch'an."

Pai Chü-i finally understood and became a true practitioner of Ch'an.

Because we still have not realized our true nature, we perceive things in this world as either good or bad, either large or small.

Thus, we make distinctions among all things.

When we practice giving, the more we give, the more merits we acquire. If we give scantily, then we will not gain much merit.

When we practice with our bodies, we can abstain from killing, stealing, and sexual misconduct. With regard to speech, we can abstain from lying, flattery, double-talk, and negative remarks. With regard to the mind, we can abstain from greed, hatred, and delusion. Consequently, there are different practices that are appropriate for the body, speech, and mind. However, for a person who has seen his or her true nature, which is originally pure and perfect, then there is no need to practice. This is the essence of Ch'an that Master Wei-k'uan had been trying to demonstrate.

What Cannot Be Stolen?

Zen Master Ryōkan of Japan lived in a small hut at the bottom of a hill. He led a simple life. One night, a thief entered his hut but found nothing worth stealing.

Upon Ryōkan's return, he bumped right into the thief.

Ryōkan said, "You might have come a long way, but I really do not have anything of value here. Yet, I cannot allow you to go back empty-handed. The only thing I have that is of value here is the shirt on my back. I will give it to you as a gift."

The thief took the shirt and left.

The half-naked Ryōkan sat down and whispered to himself, "I wish that I could give him this beautiful moon!"

People in this world use various methods to satisfy their desires. What do they really possess at the end? People come to this world empty-handed, and they will leave in the same manner. If people want to enjoy themselves, then the cool wind, the bright moon, the mountains and rivers are all here for the whole world to enjoy. Why engage in all sorts of schemes for material gains?

Just as no one can steal the moon, neither can anyone steal the Buddha-nature that is within each of us.

Don't Worry about It!

An attractive female decided to practice Ch'an so that she could become enlightened. Hence, she went to a Ch'an master and asked, "Master, what should I do to attain enlightenment?"

In ancient times, Ch'an masters employed many techniques to instruct others in the practice of Ch'an. Sometimes, they would teach someone to meditate on *kung-an*s such as "Who Is Meditating on the Buddha?" and "What Was My Original Face before My Parents Gave Birth to Me?"

The Master thought to himself: "Such an attractive young lady will encounter ample obstacles that could hinder her practice. How can she practice Ch'an so that she can become enlightened?" Then he taught her to recite, "Let it be. Don't worry about it!" The purpose of giving the lady such statements to recite was to help her concentrate so that she could see her own nature.

The lady was very serious and practiced diligently. One day, someone told her that her boyfriend had come to see her. She replied, "Let him be. Don't worry about him!"

Soon after, a university that she had applied to informed her of her admittance. She only said, "Let it be. Don't worry about it!"

Her mother called and said, "You have won the lottery jackpot."

She exclaimed, "Let it be. Don't worry about it!"

She overcame one temptation after another. One day, she came across an old photograph of her grandmother and herself when she was young. Seeing that the young girl in the picture was actually herself, she thought: "Eventually I will die and be buried just like my grandmother." Thinking such thoughts, she finally overcame the hindrance of birth and death and was no longer afraid of them. By understanding the impermanence of birth and death, she realized the bliss of no birth and no death. Her understanding of this truth is more valuable than anything else in this world.

The Entire Body Is the Eye

Ch'an Master Tao-wu asked Yün-yen, "Kuan-yin has one thousand hands and one thousand eyes. Please tell me, which eye is the real eye?"

Yün-yen then asked, "When you are sleeping at night and your pillow falls to the floor, you pick it up without opening your eyes and go back to sleep. Tell me, which eye did you use when you picked up the pillow?"

After listening to this, Tao-wu exclaimed, "Dharma brother, I understand now!"

"What do you understand?"

"The eye is the entire body."

Yün-yen smiled and said, "You only know eighty percent of it."

Tao-wu asked doubtfully, "What should I have said then?"

"The entire body is the eye!"

Saying "the eye is the entire body" is to understand through differentiation. Saying "the entire body is the eye" reveals truth through the wisdom of our minds, which make no distinctions. Our true minds are our perfect eyes; why then do we not use them to see through heaven and Earth?

The Stone Path Is Slippery

Ch'an Master Yin-fêng decided to take his leave of Ch'an Master Ma-tsu Tao-i. The latter asked, "Where are you going?"

Yin-fêng answered, "I am going to study under the guidance of Master Shih-t'ou Hsi-ch'ien of Nan-yüeh."

Ma-tsu remarked, "The stone path[24] is slippery."

Then Yin-fêng said, "The bamboo pole and wooden stick are with me, and I will play them by ear."

Ma-tsu gave Yin-fêng permission to leave, and Yin-fêng went from Kiangsi to Hunan to pay his respects to Master Shih-t'ou.

Yin-fêng walked around the Ch'an platform once, shook his monk's staff, and asked, "What is your teaching?"

Master Shih-t'ou ignored him. After a long time, Shih-t'ou said, "Good heavens! Good heavens!"

Yin-fêng could not understand his meaning and had nothing to say in reply.

Having no other alternatives, Yin-fêng returned to Master Ma-tsu and told him what had happened at his meeting with Master Shih-t'ou.

Master Ma-tsu told him, "Go back, and when Master Shih-t'ou says, 'Good heavens! Good heavens!' you should reply, 'Hiss, hiss.'"

Yin-fêng went to Nan-yüeh once more and again asked, "What is your teaching?"

Without any hesitation, Master Shih-t'ou exclaimed, "Hiss, hiss!"

Yin-fêng was again at a loss for words and returned to report to Master Ma-tsu.

Master Ma-tsu consoled him by saying, "I told you that the stone path is slippery!"

Ch'an is not something that can be imitated. It is something that we have to understand through our own minds. When Shih-t'ou said, "Good heavens! Good heavens!" he was pointing out that the teaching of Ch'an cannot be verbally described. When Yin-fêng asked him again, Master Shih-t'ou replied by hissing to show that Ch'an is something that cannot be explained by the mere use of language. Ch'an is realized through practice and not just by mere speech.

How Can Your Mind Move?

Ch'an Master Yang-shan had a Buddhist nun by the name of Miao-hsin as his disciple. Because the monk in charge of receiving guests had resigned, Yang-shan asked Miao-hsin to assume that position. Everyone at the temple felt that this was appropriate since Miao-hsin was very capable, enthusiastic, and had the courage to plunge ahead with things.

One day, seventeen monks from Szechuan arrived to pay their respects to Yang-shan and wanted to study with him.

After supper, the monks had nothing to do, so they started discussing the question of whether "the wind is moving or the banner is moving?" Since they were unable to resolve the problem amongst themselves, they argued so loudly that Miao-hsin overheard them and went in shouting, "You seventeen outsiders, make sure you settle your accounts for room and board before you leave in the morning."

Miao-hsin was so stern that the monks fell silent and did not know how to respond.

Miao-hsin ordered, "Stop arguing! Come over here, and I will tell you the answer." The monks went to Miao-hsin, who then addressed them, "Since it is neither the wind that is moving nor the banner that is moving, how can your minds move?" At that instant, all the monks attained a new insight. The following day, the monks took their leave of Miao-hsin without waiting to listen to the teaching of Yang-shan.

Once, two monks were arguing about whether the wind was moving or whether the banner was moving. The Sixth Patriarch, Hui-nêng, said to them, "It is neither the wind moving nor the banner moving. It is your minds that are moving." Miao-hsin's comment "Since it is neither the wind moving nor the banner moving, how can your minds move?" was superior compared to the response of the Sixth Patriarch.

The Sixth Patriarch advocated the integration of the objective and the subjective, whereas Miao-hsin transcended integration, asserting neither the subjective nor the objective. The implication is that when thought arises, one would be considered off track. Obviously, her understanding was higher than that of Hui-nêng.

Transcending Birth and Death

Once, when Ch'an Master P'u-hua was studying with Ch'an Master Lin-chi, he went on the street to beg for a robe. Someone offered him a robe made of the finest material, but P'u-hua would not accept it.

Master Lin-chi heard about what had happened and bought a coffin for P'u-hua. P'u-hua was very pleased with the coffin and said, "I have gotten my robe."

P'u-hua picked up the coffin, went onto the street, and began shouting, "Lin-chi has provided a robe for me. I am going to wear it for my funeral. Tomorrow morning, I shall die by the East Gate."

The next day, P'u-hua carried the coffin to the East Gate. A large crowd had already gathered to watch what was about to take place. P'u-hua announced, "There are too many people here. It is not a good place to die. I will go and die by the South Gate tomorrow."

After three days of moving from the South Gate to the West Gate and then from the West Gate to the North Gate, no longer did anyone believe Master P'u-hua's words. The people said, "We have been fooled by P'u-hua. A healthy man will not die just because he says so. We are not going to be fooled by him again tomorrow."

On the fourth day, P'u-hua carried his coffin to the North Gate. Only a few people were gathered to see what was going to occur. P'u-hua was very content and noted, "You are all very patient and have not been put off by my moving from the East to the South, West, and North. Now, I shall die for you."

After saying this, P'u-hua climbed into the coffin, closed the lid, and was never heard from again.

Average people are usually happy about living and lament when it comes to dying. For a Ch'an master, life and death can be made into a joke because one sees that life and death are one. People such as Master P'u-hua have already transcended the cycle of life and death.

He Did Not Say a Word

When Ch'an Master Huang-lung was staying at Ching-chieh Temple, he met Ch'an Master Tung-shan Yüan. Huang-lung did not say a word. The two of them burned incense and sat facing each other. They sat like this from afternoon until midnight. Finally, Master Tung-shan Yüan stood up and said, "It is getting late now, and I should not bother you while you rest." After this remark, he left.

The next day, both returned to their respective temples.

When Huang-lung returned to his temple, he asked Head Monk

Yung, "Did you meet with Master Tung-shan Yüan when you were living at Lu-shan?"

"No, I have only heard of his name." After some time, Yung continued, "Master, you met with him this time. What kind of person do you think he is?"

Huang-lung declared, "A remarkable person!"

Later, the Head Monk questioned the attendant who had accompanied Huang-lung, "You were with the Master when he met Tung-shan. What did they discuss?"

The attendant told him how the two masters sat facing each other without exchanging a word. The Head Monk took a deep breath and shouted, "People in the whole world are going to wonder!"

People exchange ideas through language. At times, language can entangle our thinking. Ch'an does not rely on spoken or written language. When Ch'an masters communicate, they may raise their eyebrows and blink their eyes. At other times, they may strike with a stick, shout, laugh, or scold others. All these are direct teaching methods. Although Huang-lung and Tung-shan did not exchange any words, they had already experienced mental communication. The Head Monk did not need to have any doubts. In any case, doubts can also lead one onto the Path of Ch'an.

Who Is in the Well?

A young novice asked Ch'an Master Hsing-kung, "What was the meaning of the Patriarch's coming from the West?"

The Master replied, "Assume someone fell into a well that is one thousand feet deep. If you can rescue him without using even an inch of rope, then I will tell you."

The novice said, "Ch'an Master Ch'ang of Hunan who passed away recently was just like you. Your style of speech is nonsensical."

Hsing-kung ordered Yang-shan to oust the novice from the temple.

Later, Yang-shan asked Ch'an Master Tan-yüan, "In your judgment, how can the man in the well be rescued?"

Tan-yüan exclaimed, "You fool! Who is in the well?"

Yang-shan was unable to respond.

Another time, he questioned Ch'an Master Kuei-shan, "Master, how do you think the man in the well can be rescued?"

Kuei-shan caught Yang-shan off guard and shouted, "Yang-shan!"

When Yang-shan responded, Master Kuei-shan said, "The man is already out."

Sometime later, when Yang-shan started to teach, he often told people, "I have received my spiritual life at Master Tan-yüan's temple and my realization at Kuei-shan's."

It is true that sometimes when Ch'an masters talk, they do not make any sense. Ch'an is beyond common knowledge. Most people's thinking is limited to concrete explanations. They do not know that this intellectual understanding is derived from the false mind and is not the true realization of the Ch'an mind.

When someone falls into a well that is one thousand feet deep, they have to be rescued by someone else; how troublesome this is [not being able to rely solely on ourselves]. However, if we can confront the problem from the standpoint of Principle, then we can pull ourselves out after falling into the well. Wouldn't the real world be ours?

Receiving Guests

The King of Chao made a special trip to visit Ch'an Master Chao-chou Tsung-shen. Chao-chou was resting in bed when the King arrived. He greeted the King from his bed, saying, "Your Majesty! I am really growing old and feeling very weak. Please, forgive me for not getting up to receive you."

Not only was King Chao not offended, but he respected Chao-chou even more.

The next day, King Chao sent a general to present some gifts to Chao-chou. Upon hearing this, Chao-chou got up from his bed and went all the way to the main gate to receive the general.

Not understanding why the Master behaved in such a manner, his disciples asked him, "Yesterday, when King Chao was here, you did not get up from your bed to receive him. Yet, when the general came today, you went all the way to the main gate to receive him. Why did you do that?"

Chao-chou explained, "You know, I have three ways of receiving guests. Superior guests, I receive in bed with my original face. Ordinary guests, I receive politely in the guest room. Inferior guests, I receive at the main gate with conventional formalities."

In the mundane world, we must differentiate between different practices in accordance with certain standards that are set forth by the society. However, Chao-chou's way of receiving guests had been derived from this Ch'an mind, so it would be considered superior to the understanding of average people. How should we behave in this world? Should we behave according to conventional principles or ultimate principles? Or should we practice both? It is something that we have to decide for ourselves.

Treasure the Present Moment

When Master Shinran was nine years old, he had already decided to become a monk. He requested Ch'an Master Jichin to tonsure him.

Master Jichin asked him, "You are so young. Why do you want to become a monk?"

Shinran answered, "Although I am only nine years old, both of my parents have already passed away. I do not understand why people must die. Why must I be separated from my parents? I want to become a monk so that I can find the answers to these questions."

Impressed, the Master said, "All right! Now that I know why you want to become a monk, I can take you as my disciple. It is getting late now. Wait until tomorrow morning, and I will tonsure you then."

Shinran disagreed, "Master! Although you have just promised to tonsure me tomorrow morning, I cannot guarantee that my determination to become a monk will last that long. Besides, you are so old now, you cannot guarantee that you will still be alive tomorrow."

Master Jichin was pleased and said, "You are right. I will tonsure you immediately!"

Master Hsüan-tsang of the T'ang dynasty was twelve when he entered the *Sangha*. At that time, anyone who wanted to enter the monastic life had to take an entrance examination. Because Hsüan-tsang was too young, he was not immediately accepted and began shedding tears of sorrow. The official in charge of the examination asked him why he insisted on becoming a monk. Hsüan-tsang answered, "To glorify the *Tathāgata*'s teaching and to continue the *bodhi* seed of the Buddha."

Despite his tender age, Hsüan-tsang was determined and was finally admitted into the *Sangha*. Later, he proved himself to be one of the greatest monastics in Chinese history. Similarly, Shinran proved to be one of the most important personalities in the history of Japanese Buddhism.

The Inside and Outside of Yün-men

Ch'an Master Yün-men made a trip to visit Ch'an Master Mu-chou. By the time he arrived, it was dusk. Yün-men knocked loudly on the door, which was already tightly shut. After a long time, Mu-chou answered the door. Yün-men explained the purpose of his visit, and as he was setting one foot inside the house, Mu-chou slammed the door on his foot.

Yün-men screamed, "Ouch! Ouch! It hurts!"

The Master asked, "Who is hurting?"

Yün-men exclaimed, "Sir, I am hurting!"

The Master inquired, "Where are you?"

Yün-men answered, "I am outside of this door!"

The Master asked, "If you are outside, why are you hurting?"

Yün-men responded, "Because you slammed the door, and my foot is caught inside."

"If your foot is inside, why are you outside?"

Yün-men replied, "You have separated me into inside and outside."

"You fool!" the Master exclaimed, "How can a person be both inside and outside?"

This question struck Yün-men's heart like a hammer. Suddenly, the world of illusion was shattered, and Yün-men became enlightened.

Although Yün-men's foot was caught, the act of slamming the door destroyed his illusions and helped him to realize non-duality and the equality of inside and outside.

To a Ch'an adept, all relative worldly concepts such as inside or outside, you or me, good or bad, big or small, and so on are illusory. Most of us are bound by these illusory concepts. When we have transcended all of these concepts, we will become enlightened.

Only Steal Once

One day, when Ch'an Master Shih-wu was traveling, he met a stranger. After talking to each other for a long time, darkness approached, so they spent the night at a guest house.

In the middle of the night, Shih-wu heard someone moving around and asked, "Is it morning already?"

The stranger said, "No, it is still night time."

Shih-wu thought to himself: "This person who can move around in the dark must be highly cultivated. Maybe he is an *arhan*."

Hence, Shih-wu asked, "Who are you?"

"I am a thief," answered the man.

Shih-wu exclaimed, "Oh! A thief! How many times have you stolen before?"

The thief replied, "Countless times."

"Each time that you have stolen, how long did you remain happy?"

The thief replied, "That depends on the value of the things I stole."

"When you were the happiest, how long did it last?"

The thief said, "It only lasted a few days."

Shih-wu concluded, "Oh! So you are just like a rat who steals a little bit at a time. Why don't you pull off a bigger job?"

The thief asked, "Have you had any experience? How many times have you stolen before?"

Shih-wu replied, "Only once."

The thief asked, "Only once and that was enough?"

Shih-wu said, "Although I did it just once, I cannot possibly spend all that I have stolen in my lifetime."

The thief asked, "What did you steal? Can you tell me?"

Shih-wu grabbed hold of the thief and said, "This! Do you understand? This is boundless treasure (the treasure that is inside each of us). If you spend your whole life and work on this, then you cannot spend it all within your lifetime. Do you understand?"

The thief said, "Yes and no. But this is a very good feeling."

The thief regretted what he had done in the past, and under Shih-wu's guidance, he eventually became a Ch'an practitioner.

How strange that people constantly chase after external goods and neglect the true treasure hidden within themselves!

Go with the Flow

When Ch'an Master Fa-yen Wen-i was practicing with Ch'an Master Ch'ing-hui, he could not attain any sort of realization and left Master Ch'ing-hui to travel like a cloud drifting throughout the four corners of the world.

Once, Fa-yen was caught in the rain, and hence, he stopped at a temple called Ti-tsang Yüan. The monk who was in charge of the visitors asked him, "Master, where are you going?"

"I don't have any place in mind. I am just wandering."

The monk asked, "How do you feel when traveling throughout the four corners of the world like clouds and water?"

Fa-yen replied, "I just go with the flow, like clouds and water."

The monk concluded, "To go with the flow, like clouds and water, this is really being carefree!"

When he heard this, Fa-yen attained a true understanding of the meaning of being carefree.

Most people in this world have to travel east, west, north, and south to make a living. How many people can really go with the flow like clouds and water, let alone be carefree?

Heaven and Hell in a Bucket of Water

A devotee asked Ch'an Master Wu-tê, "Master, I have studied Ch'an for many years, but I am still not enlightened, and I am very doubtful about the existence of heaven and hell as described in the sutras. I don't think there is a heaven and a hell beyond this world."

Master Wu-tê did not answer his question immediately. Instead, he told the devotee to go and get a bucket of water from the river.

When the devotee returned with the water, Master Wu-tê said to him, "Look inside the bucket, and maybe you will be able to see heaven and hell."

Since his curiosity was aroused, the devotee looked into the bucket, but he could not see anything. Suddenly, Master Wu-tê pushed the devotee's head into the bucket. The devotee struggled with pain. Finally, the Master released his hand when the devotee was almost out of breath. After regaining his breath, the devotee complained, "How can you be so cruel and push my head into the water? It was just like hell."

The Master said calmly, "Now, how do you feel?"

The devotee replied, "Now, I can breathe easily. It is like heaven!"

The Master ridiculed solemnly, "In only a short while, you have returned from heaven and hell, and you said that you don't believe in the existence of a heaven and a hell?"

Those who have never been to a far off country do not believe that there is such a place. This does not mean that it does not exist but merely shows that they are ignorant. Foolish people do not believe in things until they have actually seen them, whereas people who are intelligent do not necessarily have to see in order to believe. They can use their judgment to decide.

A Mouthful of Good Teeth

Master Fo-kuang had always been kind to his disciples. He saw to it that the temple took care of their welfare, including medical care, travel expenses, education, and the daily needs of all the disciples, and thus, the temple fulfilled the objective of financial equality within the monastic community.

One day, the accountant approached the Master with a stack of bills and said, "Master, many disciples have had dental problems lately. Although toothaches are not serious, they can be painful. So, we have tried our best to look after these needs. But it is just too expensive. It is very costly to just fill a few cavities. It is getting to be too much of a burden for the monastery."

The Master replied, "Although it is a burden, we still have to find some means to pay for these bills."

The accountant continued, "Some of these people are ungrateful for what we have done, but they also criticize the policies of the monastery. I think that it is not worth our while in wasting money on such people."

Master Fo-kuang mumbled to himself, "Although these people cannot speak of anything that is good, at least they should have a mouthful of good teeth."

The Buddhas and bodhisattvas sacrifice themselves to serve all beings. They not only help all beings to have a mouthful of good teeth, but they also help them to have a good heart while insuring the development of their Buddha-nature. The goal of a truly enlightened Ch'an master is to serve others; it is irrelevant whether one will be repaid.

Detachment

Ch'an Master Chin-tai liked orchids very much and planted hundreds of various species in the garden. Most of his leisure was spent tending them. One day, Master Chin-tai had to go out, and he assigned one of his disciples to water the orchids. While he was watering them, the disciple accidentally knocked down the shelf on which the orchids were placed, breaking many of the pots. The disciple thought to himself: "When the Master comes back, he will be very angry with me." There was nothing he could do except await his punishment.

When Master Chin-tai returned, not only was he not infuriated, but he even comforted his disciple by saying, "The reason I planted these orchids is because I wanted to offer them to the Buddha as well as to beautify our environment. I never planted them so that I could get angry. Everything in this world is impermanent. Attachment to the things we like is not proper conduct for a Ch'an practitioner."

In this world, the most difficult thing to do is to let go. It is equally difficult to detach ourselves from things that we like and things that we dislike. Feelings of love and hate constantly occupy our minds, so that we can never be freed. If we can become detached from the things that we like and accept the things that we dislike to the point of eliminating feelings of love and hate, then we can really be freed from all illusions and attain true liberation! Master Chin-tai didn't plant the orchids for the purpose of being infuriated is evidence that Chin-tai is a highly cultivated Ch'an master.

Hearing and Seeing

One night, Ch'an Master Ching-hsü brought a woman to his room, closed the door, and stayed alone with her. His disciple, Man-kung, afraid that other people in the temple might discover this, stood on guard outside the door. When people went to see Master Ching-hsü, Man-kung would say that the Master was resting.

Finally, he decided that this could not continue and plucked up his courage to go and talk to his master. When he entered the room, he saw a long-haired woman lying on the bed, while his master was giving her a massage.

Man-kung was shocked and hollered, "Master! How can you set such an example for us?"

Master Ching-hsü calmly asked, "Why not?"

Man-kung pointed his finger at the woman who was on the bed and said accusingly, "Look at what you are doing!"

Gently, the Master said, "Come and look."

At this point, the woman turned her head. Man-kung saw a half-rotted face and could hardly make out her eyes, nose, and mouth, because the woman had leprosy.

Man-kung knelt down and apologized, "Master, please forgive my ignorance. I cannot see what you see, nor can I do what you do."

Most people place too much faith in the veracity of what they hear and what they see. They do not know that normally what they hear and what they see are only fractions of the whole situation. If we are not careful and cling on to what we hear and what we see as the undoubted truth, then we are no better than a person who is blind or deaf.

Seeking Buddha's Path

Yang T'ing-kuang of the T'ang dynasty met with Ch'an Master Pên-ching at Szŭ-kung Shan. He implored the Master, "Birth and death are great matters. Life is impermanent and can pass away very quickly. I am single-mindedly seeking the Buddha's teaching. Please be compassionate and instruct me."

Pên-ching said, "You have come from the capital, which is the residence of the Emperor. Since there are many Ch'an practitioners at the capital, you should ask about the Buddha's teaching there. I do not know anything about the Buddha's teaching which you are seeking."

When Yang T'ing-kuang asked again, Master Pên-ching said, "If you are seeking for the Buddha, then your mind is the Buddha. If you are asking about the Buddha's teaching, then no-mind is the teaching."

Yang T'ing-kuang did not fully understand the meaning implicit in the Master's words. Therefore, he asked for further instruction.

Master Pên-ching said, "To say 'The mind itself is Buddha'[25] implies that Buddha must be realized by means of the mind. If one is further awakened into no-mind, then even Buddha ceases to exist. Thus, no-mind is none other than 'the Buddha's teaching.'"

After listening to what the Master had commented, Yang T'ing-kuang said, "Most of the monastics in the capital said that we should seek for the Buddha through the practice of generosity, morality, tolerance, and self-restraint. According to what you have said, since we all have the pure wisdom of *prajñā*, then there is no need to practice in order to attain this wisdom. If it is true, then all my generosity and moral behavior are really useless."

"Useless!" echoed Master Pên-ching.

When Bodhidharma, the first Ch'an patriarch, went to China, Emperor Wu of the Liang dynasty asked him, "I have built temples, made offerings to the *Sangha*, and propagated Buddhism. How much merit have I gained from all these acts?"

Bodhidharma answered, "There is no merit involved." He did not mean that there was no merit involved in these actions, but rather, everyone has the Buddha-nature within; it is not necessary to seek for it externally.

How do we see our own nature and attain Buddhahood? To cross to the other shore, we need to have a raft. Thus, the practices of generosity, morality, and so on are instrumental in ferrying us across to the shore of enlightenment.

What Is Being Taught?

A monk who studied the Buddhist doctrine asked Ch'an Master Ma-tsu Tao-i, "In the Ch'an tradition, what is being taught?"

Ma-tsu asked, "What do you teach?"

"I have taught more than twenty sutras and *śāstras*."

Ma-tsu exclaimed, "You must be Mañjuśrī who rode on the lion!"

The monk protested, "I dare not make such a claim."

Then Ma-tsu made a hissing sound.

The monk emphatically stated, "This is the teaching."

Ma-tsu asked, "What kind of teaching is this?"

"It is the teaching of a lion coming out of its den."

Ma-tsu remained silent.

The monk added, "Not speaking is also a kind of teaching."

"What kind of teaching is it?" inquired Ma-tsu.

"It is the teaching of a lion remaining in its den."

Ma-tsu then asked, "When there is no inside or outside, what kind of teaching is it?"

Finally, the monk could not give a response and wanted to take his leave. Ma-tsu beckoned him to approach, "Come here!"

The monk turned his head.

Then Ma-tsu asked, "What kind of teaching is this?"

Still, the monk could not answer.

Ma-tsu declared, "This is the teaching of a fool!"

Ch'an does not rely on any kind of spoken or written language. Śākyamuni Buddha taught for forty-nine years on over three hundred occasions, yet he claimed that he never uttered a word. At the same instant, he was not lying. The truth is always the truth, and talking neither increases nor diminishes it. Thousands of words are not necessarily superior to silence.

Repaying Old Debts

When Ch'an Master T'ung-hui was still a novice, his master told him to fetch some water one day. A fish peddler happened to pass by, and a fish jumped into T'ung-hui's bucket. T'ung-hui struck the fish and killed it. Later, T'ung-hui became an abbot.

One day, he said to his disciples, "A *kung-an* that had begun thirty years ago should be finished today."

His disciples asked what it was, and T'ung-hui answered, "You should know by noon."

After saying this, he closed his eyes and began meditating.

General Chang-chün, who was a devout Pure Land practitioner, was leading his soldiers through Kuanchung and was passing by Master T'ung-hui's temple.

Suddenly, Chang-chün became enraged for no apparent reason. He took his bow and arrow and stormed into the Dharma Hall, staring angrily at Master T'ung-hui.

T'ung-hui said, "I have been waiting for you for a long time."

Perplexed, Chang-chün asked, "I have never met you before. Why do I feel such anger towards you? I really want to kill you, but I do not know the reason."

Master T'ung-hui told him the story of his experience thirty years ago as a novice, when he killed a fish unintentionally.

After listening to the story, Chang-chün was moved and said:

> Taking revenge against each other,
> When is it ever going to end?
> Meeting life after life is no accident.
> We should forget our old enmities and go to
>   the Western Pure Land.

When he finished saying this, he passed away while still standing.
Later, Master T'ung-hui wrote the following on a piece of paper:

> Drifting around for thirty years,
> So much has changed.
> Who knew that we should meet today,
> Only to settle our old debts.

Upon having finished writing the above verse, he too passed away.

**"The law of cause and effect (karma) follows us like our shadow."
This is the truth!**

Good and Evil from the Same Heart

Ch'an Master Tao-hsin, the Fourth Patriarch of the Ch'an School, went to Niu-t'ou Shan to visit Fa-jung. He saw Fa-jung meditating, oblivious to his surroundings. He did not even look at the Master.

Tao-hsin went up and asked Fa-jung, "What are you doing here?"

Fa-jung answered, "I am watching my mind."

Tao-hsin asked, "Who is watching, and what is the mind?"

Fa-jung could not respond, so he rose from his seat, prostrated himself before the Fourth Patriarch, and asked, "Where is Your Venerable staying?"

Tao-hsin responded, "The place where I am going to stay is uncertain. Sometimes I go east, and sometimes I go west."

Fa-jung inquired, "Do you know Ch'an Master Tao-hsin?"

Tao-hsin asked, "Why do you ask?"

"I have heard of him and long to pay my respects to him."

Tao-hsin said, "I am Tao-hsin."

Fa-jung queried, "What brought you here?"

Tao-hsin questioned, "I came to visit. Other than this place, is there any other place where I can rest?"

Fa-jung said, "There is a small hut east of here."

Tao-hsin asked him to show the way. There were many tiger and wolf tracks around the hut. Tao-hsin made a hand gesture as if he were afraid.

Master Fa-jung queried, "You still have this (fear) with you?"

Tao-hsin questioned, "What did you just see?"

Fa-jung could not answer. He asked Tao-hsin to take a seat and went to fetch some tea. Then, Tao-hsin wrote the [Chinese] character "Buddha" on the seat opposite of his.

When Fa-jung came back and was about to sit down, he saw the character "Buddha" on his seat, so he did not dare to sit because it was considered improper and disrespectful to sit on top of the Buddha.

Tao-hsin laughed and said, "You still have this [fear] with you?"

Fa-jung did not know how to reply.

If we do not see through the illusions of birth and death, then we will continue to experience fear. If we do not see through the illusions of fame and disgrace, we will continue to experience gain and loss. If we do not see through the illusions of fame and humility, we will continue to make discriminations. If we do not see through the illusions of average people and the Buddha, we will continue to have distorted thoughts. This is the reason why Tao-hsin's state of mind was so different from Fa-jung's.

The Self-Cultivating Fellow

Master Huang-po entered the *Sangha* at a very tender age. While he was traveling on T'ien-t'ai Shan, he met a strange monk, and the two of them became friends and traveled together.

When they reached a flooded stream, the monk asked Huang-po to cross the stream with him. Then Huang-po inquired, "The stream is so deep. Are you sure we can cross it?"

The monk rolled up his pants and crossed the stream as if he was walking on flat ground. He turned around and urged, "Come on!"

Huang-po shouted after him, "Ha! You self-cultivating fellow.[26] If I had known you were like this, I would have broken your legs."

The monk was ashamed of himself and said, "You are a true Mahayanist. I cannot be compared to you." Then he disappeared.

Buddhahood will never be attained if one is only concerned with self-cultivation. For bodhisattvas who are treading on the Path of Buddhahood, helping others would always be their main concern.

Going to Hell

Someone asked Ch'an Master Chao-chou, "Master, where would a person with such perfect virtue and wisdom as yourself go when you pass away?"

Chao-chou retorted, "To hell!"

The questioner was puzzled and inquired, "How is that possible?"

Chao-chou answered, "If I don't go to hell, who is going to save you from hell?"

Chao-chou's vow to go to hell is like the great vow of Ti-tsang who stated, "If I do not go to hell, who will?" Great vows like this can only be made by people who possess great compassion.

A Dragon Gives Birth to a Dragon

Ch'an Master Tan-hsia went to visit Ch'an Master Hui-chung. When Tan-hsia arrived, Hui-chung was resting. Tan-hsia asked Tan-yüan, Hui-chung's disciple, "Is the Ch'an Master at home?"

Tan-yüan had just started to practice Ch'an and wanted to show off. Hence, he replied, "He is here, but he is not receiving any visitors."

Tan-hsia said, "Why not?"

Tan-yüan got carried away and remarked, "Even if you had the eyes of the Buddha, you could not see him."

Tan-hsia sighed and said, "A dragon gives birth to a dragon, and a phoenix gives birth to a phoenix."

When Hui-chung woke up, Tan-yüan reported to the Master about Tan-hsia's visit and their conversation. After hearing the story, he gave his disciple twenty lashes and ousted him from the temple.

When Tan-hsia heard what Hui-chung did, he was greatly impressed and said, "Hui-chung is a true Ch'an master."

Ch'an is not something which we should boast. Tan-yüan received twenty lashes for flaunting, while Tan-hsia praised Hui-chung for ousting Tan-yüan from the temple. This demonstrates that a true Ch'an adept makes no discriminations which is indeed the true art of Ch'an.

Failing to Use the Everyday Mind

A novice went to the teaching hall to ask his master, "Master, I have always meditated, chanted sutras, retired and risen early. There are no impurities in my mind. Ever since I became your disciple, no one has worked as hard as I have. Why is it that I have not attained enlightenment?"

The Master gave the novice a gourd bottle and a pinch of salt and said, "Go and fill the gourd with water and dissolve the salt in it. Then, you will attain enlightenment."

The novice did as he was instructed. He returned after a little while and said to the Master, "I put the salt into the bottle-gourd, but the salt has not dissolved. I tried to put a chopstick inside, but the mouth of the bottle-gourd is too small, and I cannot stir the water. Therefore, I still cannot attain enlightenment."

The Master picked up the bottle, poured out some water, shook it a couple of times, and the salt dissolved. Gently, the Master said to the novice, "Although you have worked diligently, if you do not use your everyday mind, how can you attain enlightenment? It is like a bottle that is filled with water. It can neither be shaken nor stirred. So how can the salt dissolve?"

The novice asked, "Do you mean that we can attain enlightenment if we do not work assiduously at it?"

The Master said, "When we practice, it is like playing a musical instrument—if you adjust the strings too tight, they will break. If you adjust them too loose, you cannot create any sounds. The middle path and the everyday mind are the basis of enlightenment."

The novice finally understood.

Accomplishments cannot be attained by persistence alone nor can mere memorization of books benefit us. It is important that we leave ourselves some room to move around and allow ourselves some time to think. Proceeding neither too rapid nor too slow, working neither obsessively nor being lackadaisical constitute the Path to enlightenment.

Wild Ducks

Once, when Ch'an Master Ma-tsu and Ch'an Master Pai-chang were outside the temple, they had seen a flock of wild ducks fly by.

Ma-tsu asked, "What are they?"

Pai-chang said, "Wild ducks."

Ma-tsu continued, "Where are they flying?"

"They've already flown past," Pai-chang replied.

After hearing this, Ma-tsu grabbed Pai-chang's nose, and Pai-chang screamed with pain.

Ma-tsu queried, "Didn't you say that they've already flown past?"

Pai-chang went back to his room and cried out loudly. Everyone asked, "What happened?"

Pai-chang answered, "Go and ask the Master."

When they went to ask Master Ma-tsu, he said, "He knows. Go and ask him."

When they returned to ask Pai-chang, they found him laughing. Everyone was bewildered and asked, "You were crying before. Why are you laughing now?"

Pai-chang said, "I was crying before, and I am laughing now."

No one understood what was happening.

The next day, when Ma-tsu had just ascended the platform to lecture, Pai-chang picked up his sitting mat and proceeded outside of the lecture hall.

Ma-tsu descended the platform and also stepped outside.

"Why did you leave when I was about to teach?"

Pai-chang answered, "Today, my nose does not hurt anymore."

"You completely understood what happened yesterday."

The reason why we are deluded is because we are separated by the relativity of time and space and confused by the transmigration of birth and death. The wild ducks did not fly by; what flew by were illusory forms. Pai-chang cried and then laughed, both of which are normal human responses. When it is time to cry, we should cry. When it is time to laugh, we should laugh. There is a saying in Ch'an: "When the great matter is not realized, we should mourn as if our parents have died. When the great matter is realized, we also should mourn as if our parents have died." Both events involve crying, but in each case, we cry for different reasons. It depends on whether we have realized our own true nature.

Upside Down Character

One day, a novice asked Ch'an Master Wu-ming, "Master, you have said that when we practice Buddhism we should make the great vow to save all beings. What if there is a person who is so evil that he can no longer be considered a person, should we save him?"

The Master did not respond immediately. In a short while, he took his pen and wrote the [Chinese] character "me" upside down and asked, "What is this?"

"This is a character that has been written upside down."

"What character is it?" inquired the Master.

The novice answered, "It is 'me.'"

"Can an upside down 'me' be considered a character?"

The novice replied, "No."

"If it is not a character, then why did you say that it is 'me'?"

Upon hearing this, the novice changed his mind and said, "Yes, it can be considered a character."

The Master challenged his response, "If you say that it is a character, then why did you say that it is upside down?"

The novice did not know how to respond to this question.

"A properly written character is a character, and an upside down character is a character," continued the Master. "You said that the character is 'me' and recognized that it is written upside down because you knew the correctly written 'me.' On the other hand, if you did not know the character, and if I have written it upside down, you could not tell the difference. If someone told you that the upside down 'me' is the character 'me,' the next time when you see a correctly written 'me,' you would think that it was upside down."

The Master further explained, "Similarly, there is no difference between a good and an evil person. Regardless whether a person is good or evil, you should help the person to bring out his or her true nature. If one is clear about one's true nature, then one's behavior would not be difficult to correct."

As Buddhists, we should not only help those who are virtuous but should help the evildoers more so. Pure lotus arises from dirty mud. Killers who lay down their knives are potential Buddhas.

Good and evil only differ by one simple thought. "Good and evil are both dharmas, but Dharma, itself, contains neither good nor evil." From the perspective of true nature, every person is worth saving.

Not Your Words

Upon arriving at Hsüeh-fêng Village, Ch'an Master Wen-yen, who wanted to visit Ch'an Master Hsüeh-fêng, met a novice and asked, "Are you going up to the mountain today?"

The novice answered, "Yes."

Hence, Master Wen-yen said, "Please take a message to Master Hsüeh-fêng for me, and don't inform him that it is from me."

The novice agreed.

Wen-yen also added, "Go to the mountain. When you see the assembly gathered for the abbot's teaching, stand up in front of him, hold your wrist, and say, 'Old man, why don't you take the iron chain off your neck?'"

The novice did as Master Wen-yen had instructed. When Master Hsüeh-fêng heard what the novice said, he came down from his seat, grabbed the novice, and said, "Speak up quickly! Speak up quickly!"

The novice could not say anything.

Hsüeh-fêng pushed him and said, "These are not your words."

The novice insisted, "They are my words."

Hsüeh-fêng loudly commanded, "Bring me the rope and stick."

The novice became afraid and confessed, "No, they are not my words. Master Wen-yen of Chekiang, who is staying at the village, told me to say them."

Upon hearing this, Hsüeh-fêng told the assembly, "Go to the village, and receive the teacher of five hundred followers."

The next day, when Hsüeh-fêng met Wen-yen, the former asked, "How were you able to arrive at this stage?"

Wen-yen simply lowered his head in response and stayed to learn from Hsüeh-fêng.

In the world of Ch'an, the real cannot be false, and the false cannot be real. Regardless if one is enlightened, one cannot escape the eyes of an enlightened person.

Let's Go!

Nobleman Lee of Lung-tê Village had great respect for Ch'an Master Shan-chao. He wanted to invite the Master to be the Abbot of Cheng-t'ien Temple. However, the Master detested the routine of administrative duties. The messenger continued to plead. Master Shan-chao questioned his disciples, "I can't really leave you and go somewhere else, yet, if I take you, you cannot catch up with me."

One of his disciples confidently said, "Master, I will go with you because I can walk eighty miles a day."

The Master shook his head and sighed, "You walk too slow. There is no way you can catch up with me."

Another disciple volunteered enthusiastically, "I will go! I can walk 120 miles a day."

The Master again shook his head, "Too slow! Too slow!"

His disciples started to wonder how fast the Master could walk.

Another disciple walked slowly to the front and prostrated before the Master, saying, "Master, I will go with you."

The Master asked, "How fast can you walk?"

The disciple answered, "As fast as you can walk."

Pleased with this response, Master Shan-chao exclaimed, "All right! Let's go!" and promptly passed away with a smile on his face.

The disciple also passed away while standing beside the Master.

True Ch'an practitioners are moved neither by fame nor by gain, nor are they afraid of birth and death. Because Shan-chao had been liberated from worldly attachments, he did not want to be an abbot.

Get Out!

Once, Ch'an Master Huang-lung Hui-nan said to a novice standing beside him, "There are hundreds and thousands of ways to attain *samādhi* and boundless ways of practice; if I told you the technique in one sentence, would you believe me?"

The novice said, "If it is the Master's teaching, wouldn't I be foolish not to believe?"

Huang-lung pointed to his left and hollered, "Come over here!"

When the novice was about to move over, Huang-lung scolded him. "Chasing after sound and form, when is it going to end? Get out!"

Another novice heard about this incident and went in to see the Master. When Huang-lung asked him the same question, the novice answered, "Wouldn't I be foolish not to believe?"

Huang-lung pointed to his right and ordered, "Come over here!"

The novice remained where he was standing.

Still, Huang-lung scolded him, "You have come to learn from me, but yet, you won't listen to what I tell you to do. What is the use of your presence? Get out!"

When a Ch'an practitioner is not enlightened, whatever he or she does would be incorrect. If one is enlightened, then the whole universe contains the Buddha's teaching.

Neither going to the right nor going to the left was correct, because the novices had not yet begun to see their true nature.

Great Courage

While Ch'an Master Yin-fêng was pushing a cart full of goods on Wu-t'ai Shan, Ch'an Master Ma-tsu Tao-i was resting in the middle of the road with his feet stretched out. Master Yin-fêng asked Ma-tsu to withdraw his feet so that he could push his cart through, but Ma-tsu said, "I will only stretch my feet and will not withdraw them."

Yin-fêng shouted, "I will only go forward and will not retreat."

Neither of them would give in.

Yin-fêng pushed his cart over Ma-tsu's legs and injured him. When Ma-tsu returned to the temple, he immediately gathered everyone at the teaching hall. He held an ax and said to the assembly, "The one who just injured my legs, come forward."

Yin-fêng went before Ma-tsu and stretched out his neck. Then Ma-tsu laid down his ax and said, "You are determined about your decision and have no doubts. Now, there is no place in this universe where you cannot go."

Yin-fêng drew back his neck, prostrated before Ma-tsu, and receded out of the room in a half-bow position.

Ma-tsu praised him, saying, "A person who can advance when it is time to advance and retreat when it is time to retreat is a true Ch'an practitioner."

Ch'an practitioners' behavior sometimes may seem very strange, but they are actually applying their practice in their everyday living. Only someone with great courage will advance when it is time to advance and retreat when it is time to retreat.

Thinking neither of Good nor of Bad

Ch'an Master Hui-nêng, the Sixth Patriarch of the Ch'an School, fled south with the robe and bowl after he inherited the teaching from Ch'an Master Hung-jên. When people heard about this, a Ch'an practitioner by the name of Chen Hui-ming chased after Hui-nêng. As soon as he had caught up with him, Chen Hui-ming said that he had come only for the Dharma and not for the robe and bowl. He begged Hui-nêng to impart the Dharma to him.

Hui-nêng said, "If you really have come for the Dharma, you should give up all attachments and delusory thinking, then I will teach you the Dharma." After a while, Hui-nêng asked, "When you are thinking neither of good nor of bad, at this very moment, what is your original face?"

Upon hearing this, Hui-ming attained realization. He further implored Hui-nêng to impart to him the profound teachings. Hui-nêng answered, "If I can tell you, then it is not profound. If you can seek from within, then the profound teaching lies within your own heart."

Hui-ming was moved and said, "I have been under the guidance of Master Hung-jên for a long time, yet I never knew my true self. Now, I finally understand myself, 'like someone who drinks water and knows the coldness and warmth for oneself.'"

Hui-ming attained realization from the words taught to him by Hui-nêng. If he had not been practicing under the guidance of Hung-jên, then he probably would not have attained realization. The present moment is actually a continuation of the past. Phenomena of any sort will not occur if the right conditions are not present.

Emptiness and Non-existence

One day, Ch'an Master Fo-yin was expounding the Dharma. Su Tung-p'o heard about it and rushed over to attend the lecture, but all the seats were occupied. The Master noticed this and said, "All the seats are taken. I'm afraid there's no room for you, Mr. Su."

Su immediately retorted, "Since there are no seats here, I'll use your body which is composed of the four elements[27] and the five aggregates[28] as my seat."

Sensing that Su Tung-p'o was challenging him to a Ch'an debate, Fo-yin said, "Mr. Su! I have a question for you. If you can answer it, the body of this old monk will be your seat. If you can't, you'll have to leave your jade belt at the temple." Su was highly confident that he could answer any question, so he accepted the challenge.

Master Fo-yin asked, "Since the four elements are empty and the five aggregates are nonexistent,[29] where will you sit?"

Since the physical body is composed of substances that ultimately have no material reality, how can we sit on it? Thus, Su lost his jade belt, which remains to this day in Chin-shan Temple.

You Do Not Have the Buddha-nature

When Master Hui-lang first paid his respects to Ch'an Master Ma-tsu, the latter asked him, "Why did you come here?"

"For the knowledge of the Buddha," answered Hui-lang.

"But the Buddha has transcended knowledge," retorted Ma-tsu. "Only devils have it."

Upon hearing this, Hui-lang respectfully prostrated to Ma-tsu.

"From where did you come?" asked Master Ma-tsu.

"Nan-yüeh." [This meant that he was a disciple of Master Shih-t'ou Hsi-ch'ien of Nan-yüeh in Hunan.[30]]

Bluntly, Ma-tsu declared, "You belong in Nan-yüeh. You're unworthy of your master, Shih-t'ou. You'd better go back immediately. There is no other place that is suitable for you."

When Hui-lang returned to Nan-yüeh, he asked Shih-t'ou, "How can I attain Buddhahood?"

"You don't have the Buddha-nature," the Master answered.

"But all sentient beings have it, even worms. Why don't I?" asked the baffled Hui-lang.

"Because you're not a sentient being."

"Are you saying that I'm inferior to a worm?" queried Hui-lang.

"Yes," confirmed the Master, "because you refuse to take any responsibilities."

Hui-lang finally became enlightened by the Master's words.

It is very important for Ch'an practitioners to have confidence both in themselves and in the communities where they study Buddhism. Some people trust neither themselves nor the place where they practice. Instead, they run blindly about here and there. It is only after they have finally returned home do they realize that what they have been searching from afar can be found easily at home.

In this world, we should first know ourselves and have faith in ourselves and our vocations. We should avoid running from one place to another simply because we are not given an important position. If we accomplish nothing, it is because we refuse to take the responsibility.

Form and Emptiness Are the Same

Once, a novice asked Ch'an Master Chao-chou, "What's the meaning of 'form is emptiness, and emptiness is form'?"

Chao-chou answered, "Listen to this verse:

> Obstacles are not walls,
> Nor are places without obstacles empty;
> If you understand this,
> You know form and emptiness are by nature
>   the same."

Seeing that the novice was still puzzled, Ch'an Master Chao-chou continued:

> The Buddha-nature manifests itself in all its
>   dignity;
> But conscious beings hardly understand the
>   nature of existence.

Once they are awakened to the nonsub-
stantiality of self,
They see that there is no distinction between
the Buddha's face and their own.

Still perplexed, the novice monk queried, "But Master! What is the implication behind 'form is emptiness, and emptiness is form'?"

Opening his eyes widely, the Master declared, "Form is emptiness, and emptiness is form!"

Upon hearing this, the novice monk finally attained realization.

All material substances in the universe are called "form," but form is a product of causal conditions. It has no independent existence, and thus, it has no true nature that can be grasped. Emptiness is not the absence of matter, but rather, a void that can embrace everything. As the sutras state: "True emptiness does not hinder existence; existence does not hinder emptiness."

Unenlightened beings remain attached to the notion that the phenomenal world has an ultimate reality. Thus, they will encounter obstructions everywhere because the true implication of "form is emptiness" is not understood. As soon as people realize that form is without an inherent self and that form arises from conditioned co-production, then they will understand the implication of "there is no distinction between the Buddha's face and their own."

I-hsiu Eating the Honey

When I-hsiu was a young novice, he already demonstrated great potential for Ch'an. Once, a lay Buddhist gave his master a jar of honey. It just so happened that the Master had to go out that day. Worried that I-hsiu might eat the honey on the sly, the Master warned, "I-hsiu! A devotee has just given us this jar of poison. It's very dangerous. Be sure not to eat it."

I-hsiu was very clever and immediately saw through this gimmick. After the Master left, he ate the bottle of honey. Satiated and content, he began to think about how he would justify his conduct. Suddenly, he had an inspiration. He grabbed his master's most treasured vase and shattered it.

When the Master returned, I-hsiu laid down on the ground and cried loudly, "Master! I have committed an unpardonable sin."

"What did you do?" asked the Master.

"I've broken your prized vase!" cried I-hsiu.

"How could you be so careless?" chided the Master.

Feigning remorse, I-hsiu replied, "Master! I know that I shouldn't have broken your vase. To express my deep regret, I have committed suicide. I must tell you that I ate that jar of poison!"

Not knowing whether to laugh or to cry, the Master had to suffer in silence!

When Ch'an is applied as a means of self-cultivation, it can enlighten the mind as well as enable one to behold one's own Buddha-nature. Ch'an is also eminently useful in other contexts of life. Ch'an is wisdom—a supreme wisdom which can be humorous as well. At a young age, I-hsiu was so clever that he could make amends for his offense. Does this not demonstrate the humor of Ch'an?

Night Roving

In the temple where Ch'an Master Hsien-yai lived, there was a novice who often stealthily climbed over the courtyard wall at night in search of excitement. Only when the Master found a tall stool near the wall during his rounds one night did he realize that someone had sneaked out of the temple. Not awakening anyone, Hsien-yai quietly removed the stool and waited in its place.

Late that night, the novice returned. Expecting the stool to be where he had left it, he climbed over the wall, unknowingly stepped on the Master's head, and jumped off. When he realized that his master was standing there, he was so frightened that he did not know what to do. However, the Master was not the least bit offended. Instead, he comforted him by saying, "It's late and is getting chilly. Take good care of your health. Go and put on more clothes, or you'll catch a cold."

No one else in the temple knew of this incident, nor did Master Hsien-yai ever mention it afterward. From that time onward, none of the more than one hundred novices in the temple ever went out at night in search of excitement again.

Love is the best way of teaching. Substituting encouragement for accusation and loving care for punishment are the most effective ways to educate!

Ch'an masters like Hsien-yai exemplify the educational method of the Ch'an School in its highest form. The Ch'an School takes compassion and skillful means as its first principles. Even when scolding, beating, or disciplining students, the masters identify their fundamental potentials and limitations first and then adapt their teaching to the unique needs of each student. Parents and teachers, who follow the model set by Ch'an masters, will find that persuasion, compassion, and being a role model are the most effective educational techniques. Parents and teachers should first identify the children's nature and character and teach them accordingly.

Getting to the Root

Master Wen-shu Hsin-tao was a Ch'an practitioner. For many years, he had meditated on "The three worlds are nothing but a manifestation of the mind, and the ten thousand dharmas arise from consciousness." Not being able to attain any realization, Hsin-tao started to travel far and wide to consult other Ch'an masters.

One day, he went to the temple of Ch'an Master T'ai-p'ing Fo-chien. Hsin-tao wanted to discuss the *kung-an* "The Cypress in Chao-chou's Front Yard" with the Master in hope of receiving some instruction. Before reaching T'ai-p'ing, he ran into Master Chih-chüeh T'ieh-tsui, who had already known Hsin-tao's intention.

Chih-chüeh said, "The late Master Chao-chou didn't tell such a story. You should not make such false accusations about the Master."

Hsin-tao was puzzled by this statement. Eventually, he began to understand. One day, Hsin-tao went to the abbot's room to call on Master Fo-chien and discuss what he had learned. However, when the

Master heard Hsin-tao's footsteps, he closed the door on him.

From outside the door, Hsin-tao hollered, "Master! Don't lie to me. I know you're inside."

Fo-chien answered from within, "There's no wall to block any of the ten directions. Why don't you come in?"

After hearing this, Hsin-tao smashed through the paper covering the lattice window with his fist. Master Fo-chien abruptly flung open the door, grabbed Hsin-tao, and exclaimed, "Out with it! Out with it!"

Hsin-tao spat on the Master's face and recited the following verse:

> Chao-chou had a story about a cypress;
> Ch'an Buddhists have passed it on from one
>   another throughout the land.
> But most of them have just picked leaves or
>   twigs,
> And failed to reach the roots.
> Chih-chüeh said their version of the story was
>   not what had been told by Chao-chou;
> This was a direct reproach to them.
> If Ch'an practitioners are enlightened,
> They surely can distinguish between the true
>   and the false.

Fo-chien said approvingly, "Now you're awakened to the Truth!"

Both right and wrong and true and false exist in this world. The Cypress in Chao-chou's Front Yard" is a *kung-an* which originated in a conversation between a monk and Chao-chou. The monk asked the Master, "What was the meaning of the Patriarch's coming from the West?" Chao-chou replied, "The cypress in the front yard." The implication underlying his reply was that the cypress turned green and red according to the different seasons. The Patriarch's purpose in coming from the West was to instill this state of no-mind. Master Hsin-tao found the root of the cypress and experienced the nondiscriminating mind under the guidance of Master Fo-chien. Hence, he condemned all garrulous monks for their imperfect understanding.

Before Going Up the Tree

One day, Ch'an Master Hsiang-yen Chih-hsien, from Shantung, was giving the following instruction in the preaching hall:

There was once a monk who wanted to attain enlightenment. To do this, he stayed up on a tree solely by gripping a branch with his teeth. He didn't grasp or step on any other branches. Suddenly, someone from down below asked him, "What was the meaning of the Patriarch's coming from the West?" If he didn't answer the question, he would violate his obligation as a monk to compassionately teach others. But if he did answer, he would fall and be killed. Under such circumstances, what should he do?

All the monks who were present stared at each other, speechless. Seeing that no one could answer the question, a senior monk named Hu-t'ou Chao stood up and said, "Suppose we don't pose the question from the perspective of the monk on the tree, but rather, before the monk climbed up the tree? What would the Master say then?"

Master Chih-hsien laughed heartily and responded with a verse:

> A fully-developed chick inside an egg felt its
> protective shell was now an obstacle;
> It broke the shell from within, while the hen
> pecked it from outside.
> Later neither of them remembered how the
> shell was broken;
> But the whole process occurred in accordance
> with conditioned co-production.
> Though all monks joined in the discussion,
> Only one presented an ingenious answer to the
> question.

Master Chih-hsien's question was odd and difficult to answer. Understanding Ch'an sometimes involves giving flexible answers to avoid absorbing intellectual concepts without assimilating existential insight. Master Hu-t'ou Chao answered the question flexibly by suggesting that the monk be asked to explain the meaning of the Patriarch's coming from the West before he climbed the tree. If the essence of a question is grasped, why should one be preoccupied

with details? This is similar to hatching chicks; it does not make any difference whether the baby chick or the hen pecks the shell of the egg. The most important thing is that a new life is born. Thus, if the monastics understand the meaning of the Patriarch's coming from the West, why should they care whether they learned it from someone who was on a tree?

Only Partial Agreement

Ch'an Master Tung-shan Liang-chieh attained enlightenment under the guidance of Master Nan-ch'üan P'u-yüan. On the anniversary of the death of Tung-shan's former teacher, Master Yün-yen T'an-sheng, Tung-shan laid offerings on the altar as a commemoration. A novice monk asked, "What teaching did you obtain from your former teacher?"

Tung-shan answered, "Even though I was his disciple, he didn't give me any instruction."

"Then why do you still revere and make offerings to him?"

"How do I dare show him disrespect?" Tung-shan contemplated.

"But you have attained enlightenment under the supervision of Master Nan-ch'üan," said the novice. "I don't understand why you still make offerings to Yün-yen."

Gently, Tung-shan explained, "I don't venerate either his ethics or his Dharma. I simply respect him for not disclosing everything to me. Because of this, I think that he was kinder to me than my parents."

The novice continued, "Since you make offerings to him, you must agree with his method of Ch'an."

Tung-shan replied, "I partially agree."

"Why don't you agree completely?" asked the novice.

"Because if I do, I will disappoint him," said Tung-shan.

Master Tung-shan Liang-chieh became enlightened when he saw his reflection in the water right after his teacher, Yün-yen, had passed away. His enlightenment verse was as follows:

Guard against searching in other places;
Otherwise, you will become ever further

estranged from yourself.
Today, when I strolled along the water,
I found myself mirrored in it.
The reflection was me,
But I was not the reflection.
Due to self-attained realization,
My mind is in harmony with my teacher's.

Although Tung-shan's enlightenment took place after the death of his teacher, he did not forget the favors he had received and made offerings on the anniversary of his teacher's death. He was grateful to the teacher for not having revealed everything to him and for giving him the opportunity to attain enlightenment on his own. If one is completely dependent on one's teachers, one will become lost. On the other hand, one should not become so independent that one refuses guidance. For without the finger pointing at the moon, how can one see it?[31] Thus, the real meaning of Tung-shan's partial agreement with the teacher is that teachers should only serve as a guide to the student during the learning process.

The Virtuous Ones

Hao-yüeh once asked Ch'an Master Chao-chou, "Have all the virtuous ones[32] in the world attained nirvana?"

Chao-chou asked him in turn, "Are you asking if they've attained nirvana or if they're still in the process leading to it?"

"The former," said Hao-yüeh.

"Then they haven't attained realization yet," declared Chao-chou.

"Why not?" inquired Hao-yüeh.

"Because they haven't put as much diligence into their practice as the ancestral patriarchs had," Chao-chou replied.

"If that's the case," Hao-yüeh asked pointedly, "why are they still considered to be the virtuous ones?"

"Because they've enlightened their minds and are able to behold their own Buddha-nature and to comprehend the Buddha-wisdom. Thus, they may also be considered the virtuous ones."

Hao-yüeh persisted, "I still don't know how much earnest effort is sufficient before one can attain nirvana."

In response, Chao-chou chanted this verse:

> The luminescence of great Wisdom,
> The Path to the freedom of nirvana,
> When earnest effort is sufficient,
> Eternal light of serenity will be attained.

Hao-yüeh said, "Thank you for your explanation of the three virtues[33] of nirvana. But what is the process that leads to it?"

"Yourself!" exclaimed Chao-chou.

For Buddhist practitioners who have not attained realization, "The virtuous ones" are indispensable. According to the Buddha, being acquainted with such people is a necessary condition for enlightenment.

In the present period of degeneration of the Buddha's teaching,[34] it is very difficult to find someone who is absolutely virtuous or who has realized nirvana. Thus, one should learn from those who understand and promote the Dharma even slightly better than oneself. Moreover, one should respect and be obedient to them. The sutras state: "If one harbors ill will, resentment, or hatred toward one's teacher, it is impossible to achieve merit and religious prowess."

The sutras also declare: "Even if a person has only a few virtues that engender merit, we should still learn from them." In other words, those who continue to cultivate themselves in order to realize nirvana can become virtuous even if they have not yet accumulated much merit. Thus, Chao-chou told Hao-yüeh that Hao-yüeh, himself, was such a person.

Is It Evil or Virtue?

Master Chien-yüan Chung-hsing was an attendant of Ch'an Master Tao-wu. Once, he brought a cup of tea to Tao-wu who pointed to the cup and asked, "Is it evil or virtue?"

Chung-hsing moved closer and was face-to-face with Master Tao-wu, but he did not say a word.

Tao-wu then said, "Evil is always evil, while virtue is always virtue."

Chung-hsing shook his head by saying, "I don't think so."

"Why not?" queried Tao-wu.

Chung-hsing snatched the cup away from Tao-wu and loudly retorted, "Is it evil or virtue?"

Tao-wu clapped his hands and laughed heartily, exclaiming, "You're worthy of being my attendant!" Chung-hsing then prostrated to Master Tao-wu.

The point behind Tao-wu's question "Is it evil or virtue?" is that when an evil person talks about a law that is just, the law becomes evil, whereas when a virtuous person discusses an evil law, that law is transformed into something virtuous. There are those who are always talking about the Truth, yet, in practice, they often undermine people's faith. There are others who fight and curse; nonetheless, they can guide people in becoming good Buddhists. Similarly, good doctors can turn poison into medicine for those who are sick.

Master Chung-hsing's answer to the question was more profound. He held: "Form arises and becomes extinct according to causal conditions." If one has this understanding, one would believe that neither material substance was eternal, nor could it be annihilated. Hence, from this perspective, all substances are virtuous. If one believes that material substances, like the teacup held in the hand, are either existent or nonexistent, then every substance is evil. Chung-hsing responded by restating the question, revealing his insightful discernment of reality.

Master Tao-wu was pleased and complimented his disciple, so they have achieved a mutual understanding.

He Already Said Thank You

One night, Ch'an Master Ch'i-li was chanting when a robber with a sharp knife broke into the house and threatened the Master. "Give me your money, or I'll kill you!" demanded the robber.

Without turning around, the Master said calmly, "Don't disturb me. The money is in the drawer over there. Go and get it yourself."

The robber took all the money and was about to run away when the Master said, "Don't take it all. Leave some for me to buy flowers and fruit as offerings to the Buddha."

As the robber was about to leave, the Master said, "After accepting another's money, won't you even say 'thank you' before you go?"

Later, the robber was arrested for other crimes. During the interrogation, he confessed that he had also stolen money from Master Ch'i-li. When the police asked the Master for confirmation, he said, "He didn't rob me. I gave him the money. I remember that he even said 'thank you' to me."

The robber was greatly moved by this. After serving his sentence, he converted to Buddhism and became a disciple of Master Ch'i-li.

The teaching offered by Ch'an is dynamic. Ch'an has the power to inspire others as well as to give a person the capability of realizing the true nature within oneself.

I Cannot Tell You

A novice monk was on his way to see Ch'an Master Fu-ch'uan when he met an old man who sold salt for a living. Since the novice was not sure how to reach his destination, he asked the old man, "Grandpa! Could you tell me which road leads to Fu-ch'uan [literally meaning 'an overturned boat']?" After waiting for some time, without receiving any answer, the novice again asked the old man.

"I've already told you," replied the old man. "Are you deaf?"

"What was your reply?" the puzzled novice queried.

Then the old man said, "The road leading to Fu-ch'uan."

"Do you mean you also know Ch'an? Is that what you're talking about?"

"Yes. Not only do I understand Ch'an, but I also understand the Dharma," replied the old man.

"Would you like to discuss it with me?" asked the novice.

The old man did not answer. Instead, he put the basket of salt on his shoulder and prepared to leave.

The novice could not understand what the old man meant and sighed, "Difficult!"

"Why do you say that?" asked the old man.

"Salt seller!" the monk called out.

"Yes, what can I do for you?" responded the old man.

"What is your name?" asked the novice.

"I can't tell you that this is salt," the old man replied.

The novice intended to go to study with Master Fu-ch'uan. How could he get there? If Fu-ch'uan means "an overturned boat," how can there be a road leading to it? Various paths exist in the world, some easy and some difficult, some wide and some narrow, some monastic and some secular. While ordinary practitioners have to progress along an established route, Ch'an practitioners "with lofty aspirations would not even take the Path that the *Tathāgata* took." Thus, even in "an overturned boat," why can't there be a road?

Thick Bamboo Cannot Stop Water

A novice monk wanted to take leave of Ch'an Master Lo-p'u to study elsewhere. When he stated his intention, the Master asked, "We're surrounded by mountains. Where are you going?"

The novice was speechless.

Master Lo-p'u then said, "If you can come up with an answer in ten days, you may leave as you wish."

The novice thought hard day and night. One day, as he was pacing up-and-down in the courtyard, he ran into Master Shan-ching, who was in charge of the vegetable garden.

"I heard that you wanted to leave. Why are you still here?"

The novice told him how he had failed to answer Master Lo-p'u's question and thus had to stay.

"I can help you with the answer," offered Shan-ching, "But you mustn't tell the Master that you've learned it from me."

Overjoyed, the novice promised to keep silent.

Shan-ching said slowly and clearly, "Even a thick bamboo forest can't stop water from trickling through; how can high mountains restrain clouds from floating?"

When Master Lo-p'u heard this response from the novice, he asked, "Who told you the answer?"

"No one," the novice said, "I thought of it by myself."

"I don't believe you," said Lo-p'u, glaring back at him with his eyes wide open.

Now the novice was forced to admit the truth.

That same night, during the evening lecture, Master Lo-p'u told the assembly, "Don't underestimate the superintendent of the vegetable garden. Some day, he'll have five hundred followers!"

Later, when Master Shan-ching was promoting the Buddha's teaching in other places, he did indeed have more than five hundred disciples.

Those who really embody the Truth would never flaunt their wisdom. In a Ch'an monastery, many of those who tend the kitchen fire, fetch water, cook, or do other forms of manual labor have discerned their Buddha-nature through their work. Their true value often is overlooked. People should realize there is no such thing as a lowly task because all jobs are noble. Nonetheless, the degree to which people are awakened to the Truth varies.

Someone Else Has Borrowed It

Two novice monks from the same monastery, who had not seen each other for a long time, met. One asked the other, "I haven't seen you for ages. What have you been doing lately?"

"I've been busy making a seamless pagoda[35]," said his friend.

Pleased to hear this [but failing to understand the true meaning of a "seamless pagoda"], the first novice exclaimed, "Wonderful! I'm also thinking of making one. May I use yours as a model?"

"Why didn't you tell me earlier? Someone else has borrowed it," the second novice answered.

The first novice [understanding the meaning of their exchange] said confidently, "That's all right. I'll just take a good look at you."

The statement "I'll just take a good look at you" has the implication that the Buddha-nature within all sentient beings is the true "seamless pagoda." There is no other that exists.

The spiritual relics of the Buddha represent the complete Dharma-nature. These are the Dharma-words, the teachings of the Buddha revealed by his enlightened mind. As such, they are the embodiment of Truth. As the sutras state: "Wherever there are discourses of the Buddha, they exist as pagodas."

Since the second novice understood that the spiritual body of the Buddha was boundless, he was making a seamless or boundless pagoda as an instrument of worship. This enlightenment cannot be imitated, learned, or borrowed from anywhere or anyone. It can only be realized through personal experience. Therefore, the second novice had to use the excuse that the pagoda had been borrowed by someone else when his friend wanted to borrow it. Enlightenment, or one's own Buddha-nature, cannot be borrowed. The first novice had already realized this as well. Cultivation depends on oneself. Imitation involves merely repeating the words of others, like a parrot, without having an understanding of their implication.

My Son—T'ien-jan

Ch'an Master Hsing-ssŭ had a disciple, Tan-hsia T'ien-jan, who originally had been trained as a scholar. Tan-hsia had planned to take the imperial examinations in the capital to pursue a career as an official. He changed his mind after someone suggested, "Why don't you change your plan from pursuing an official career to becoming a Buddha?"

Tan-hsia asked, "Where should I go to accomplish this goal?"

The man suggested, "Master Ma-tsu in Kiangsi is a good choice."

Tan-hsia went there immediately. As soon as he saw the Master, he patted his head to indicate that he wanted to become a monk.

Ma-tsu told him, "The condition for you to attain realization is not here. You should go to Master Shih-t'ou."

Tan-hsia followed the Master's recommendation and went to see Master Shih-t'ou Hsi-ch'ien, who had instructed him to engage in manual labor.

One day, Shih-t'ou asked everyone to weed the area in front of the hall. Tan-hsia got a basin of water and washed his head with it. He then knelt before Shih-t'ou, with a razor in his hand.

Shih-t'ou understood his meaning, and so he tonsured him.

After that, Tan-hsia went back to see Ma-tsu. Rather than going to the reception room, he went directly to the meditation hall. There he sat astride the statue of Bodhidharma. The others who were present took him for a blasphemous roving monk and immediately sent word to Ma-tsu. When the Master came and saw this, he was pleased and said, "My son, T'ien-jan!"

Tan-hsia jumped off the statue and prostrated himself before the Master. From then on, he adopted T'ien-jan as his name.[36]

This same T'ien-jan once warmed himself in a temple by burning a statue of the Buddha, and he said that he was gathering the relics of the Buddha (a sacrilegious act).

Some Ch'an students can comprehend and experience the Dharma as soon as they are exposed to it. Others never realize the Truth, even after a lifetime of diligent study. The difference has much to do with cultivation in one's previous life and does not reflect one's cleverness or dullness in attaining enlightenment.

In the study of Buddhism, one should follow Master T'ien-jan's example by not allowing the golden opportunity to slip by. One should also guard against becoming overanxious or seeking quick results. It takes innumerable lifetimes to attain the Path of the bodhisattvas.

The Supreme Dharma

Ch'an Master Fo-kuang once presented the following to his novices:

In ancient times, people used paper lanterns with candles inside to light the road. One day, a blind man went to visit a friend. When he was about to leave, it was already dark, so his friend offered him a lantern. The man politely declined his kindness, saying, "I don't need it. To me, there is no difference between darkness or light."

The friend explained, "I know that you don't need it. But if you don't have a lantern, others may bump into you. Therefore, you had better take it with you."

This sounded reasonable, so the blind man left with the lantern. However, before he had gone very far, someone bumped into him. He yelled at the man, saying, "What's the matter with you? Didn't you see my lantern?"

The man apologized, explaining, "But brother! Your candle has gone out."

The blind man retorted, "It is the light in your mind that has gone out. How can you blame my candle?"

For those who can behold their own Buddha-nature, there is no difference between bright wisdom and dark ignorance. Although darkness may cause difficulties, doesn't the bright sun also scorch people? Even so, one can still hold a lantern, that is the torch of wisdom, to compassionately enlighten the minds of all beings.

In the endless chain of transmigration, all sentient beings cling to the concept of the self-ego and dwell in eternal darkness. Although they have two eyes, they fail to see their fellow travelers, and yet, they blame the blindness on others. How much more lamentable is the fact that the lamps of their minds have gone out. Worldly people, lacking comprehension of the Dharma, misinterpret and slander the Three Precious Ones. This is just like the sighted person who bumped into the blind man and blamed the blind man for not lighting his lantern.

The Illiterate Monk

There was a monk who meditated every day in the library containing the sutras. However, he had never read any of the sutras that were there. One day, the librarian asked him, "I noticed that you meditate here everyday. Why don't you read the sutras?"

The monk replied frankly, "Because I'm illiterate."

"Why don't you ask someone for help?" urged the librarian.

"But whom can I ask?" he inquired.

"You can ask me!" answered the librarian bluntly.

Upon hearing this, the monk stood up and prostrated. Then, with his hands held together and fingers interlaced, he asked, "What is this, if I may ask?"

The librarian had nothing to say in reply. "This" referred to our true nature. How could the librarian use words to express it precisely?

The Ch'an School does not rely on any scriptures as its basis of teaching, because our limited language cannot describe the ultimate character of the Buddha-nature.[37] The Sixth Patriarch, Hui-nêng, understood the sutras and explained their essence even before he went to study at Huang-mei, although he had not yet attained realization. Later, when he met the Fifth Patriarch, he was assigned to work in the mill everyday. Eventually, he became enlightened without studying any scriptures. Therefore, realization is not attained merely through the studying of scriptures.

The illiterate monk could not read the sutras. Nonetheless, he sat in meditation in the library every day and practiced diligently. The librarian kindly urged him to overcome his illiteracy, but the monk responded by referring to the realm of realization. Ch'an is not confined to any scriptures. If one meditates diligently, one can also behold one's own Buddha-nature.

Where Can One Dwell in Peace?

Once, Ch'an Master Tan-hsia of the T'ang dynasty went to visit Master Ma-tsu. On his way, he met a white-haired old man and a boy. Seeing that the elderly man bore himself with great dignity, the Master approached him and asked respectfully, "Where do you live, sir?"

The old man pointed up and down and then replied, "Heaven is above, and earth is below." This statement simply implies that one's home can be anywhere in the universe.

Tan-hsia, thinking he had found the old man's point of vulnerability, immediately retorted, "What if heaven collapses and the earth caves in?" [In other words, what would happen if the universe were to be destroyed?]

The old man called out, "Good heavens! Good heavens!" implying that the universe has four periods—origination, duration, degeneration, and dissolution.

At this point, the lad uttered, "Shhh," which means that the concepts of a beginning and an end cannot be applied to the place where one's own Buddha-nature dwells.

Upon hearing this, Tan-hsia praised them in a loud voice, "Like father, like son."

The old man and the boy continued their journey into the mountains.

Where can one dwell in peace? Master Tz'ŭ-hang once stated, "If one feels mentally at peace, it does not make a difference whether it is east, west, north, or south, anywhere is a fine place to dwell." Thus, with heaven above and earth below, one's home is nowhere and everywhere.

People in the world focus their lives on materialism, personal interests, fame, and power. They do not realize that all such matters are in constant flux. Therefore, how can they dwell in peace?

If people can sustain themselves and avoid being controlled by the five desires and the six dusts,[38] their minds will be at peace. Then, how does the collapse of heaven and earth concern them?

The pure moon, which is often used as a symbol of the Enlightened One, travels in the state of ultimate emptiness. It seems dangerous for the moon not to have anything on which to lean.

Actually, it is very safe because by dwelling in the infinite space of wisdom, the Buddha is truly liberated from care and worry.

A Room with Six Windows

Ch'an Master Yang-shan once asked Master Hung-ên, "Why can't we recognize our own nature more quickly?"

Hung-ên answered, "I have a metaphor for you. There is a room with six windows. A monkey inside the room is cavorting about, while five other monkeys are outside chasing the monkey which is inside the room. It is difficult for the monkey to recognize which is its own self, since one of the monkeys from outside will respond each time it calls."

After hearing this, Yang-shan realized that Hung-ên's story implied that our six sense organs—the eyes, ears, nose, tongue, body, and mind—are chasing the six dusts—sight, sound, smell, taste, touch, and consciousness. They provoke each other and become entangled. They continually move in concert with one another, like the stars in the sky. In such a situation, how can people recognize their true self?

Yang-shan then stood up and prostrated, saying, "I'm very grateful to you for having instructed me by means of this metaphor. If the monkey inside is asleep, will those outside awaken it?"

Master Hung-ên stood up and took a hold of Yang-shan's hand, using hand gestures as he spoke, "A scarecrow in a field keeps birds from eating the kernels of rice. Therefore, if a wooden figure is looking at flowers and birds, how can the thousands of things surrounding it be a source of temptations?" This answer served as a guide for Yang-shan's realization.

Why can't we recognize our own nature? It is because our true minds have long been blocked by the passions of the senses. This situation is like that of a shiny mirror covered with dust; it cannot manifest its natural luster. When our true minds fail to appear, false thoughts manipulate us. We remain attached to the six dusts and become restless and frivolous. The human body is like a village. The villagers (the mind) are imprisoned while the six bandits (the six sense organs) occupy the village, chase after the six dusts, and

fan the flames of disorder. Seeing this state of affairs through the
six windows, how can the villagers (the mind) be at peace?

Eating and Dressing

Someone asked Ch'an Master Mu-chou, "We have to eat and dress
every day. These tasks have to be repeated endlessly. They're really
bothersome. How can we rid ourselves of these burdens?"

Master Mu-chou replied, "By eating and dressing."

"I don't see what you mean," said the questioner.

"If you don't understand me, then you should eat and dress," said
Mu-chou, with an air of curt finality.

**Ch'an is not detached from life. Average people need to eat and
dress, and this applies to those who have attained enlightenment as
well. The only difference lies in the significance that people are very
much attached to eating and dressing. According to a Chinese
verse: "The moon outside the window is always the same, but it
looks more brilliant when the plum flowers are in bloom."**

All the Flavors in One

When Ch'an Master Yün-yen T'an-sheng first visited Master Yao-shan,
the latter asked, "From where have you come?"

"I came from Ch'an Master Pai-chang Huai-hai."

"What did Pai-chang teach you?" asked Yao-shan.

"He had said, 'I have a sentence that contains all the flavors.'"

Yao-shan said, "Salty is salty while bland is bland. Neither
saltiness nor blandness is the standard flavor. So what is the one
sentence that contains all the flavors?"

Master T'an-sheng had nothing to say in reply.

Yao-shan continued, "I also have a sentence: What can you do about life or death at this instant?"

"There is no life or death at this instant," retorted T'an-sheng.

"How long did you stay with Master Pai-chang?"

"Twenty years," replied T'an-sheng.

"After twenty years, you still haven't rid yourself of your worldly[39] character," concluded Yao-shan.

A few days later, Master Yao-shan again asked T'an-sheng, "Besides 'the sentence that contains all the flavors,' what did Master Pai-chang teach you about the Dharma?"

"Sometimes he would say three sentences but would ask us to leave out six."

"He and I are three thousand miles away from each other, and I'm happy we don't have any contact," said Yao-shan.

Obviously pleased, Yao-shan continued, "What else did he say about the Dharma?"

"During meditation," T'an-sheng replied, "he would sometimes wait until everyone was seated, drive us out of the room with his monk's staff, and would call us back immediately afterward. However, he would not tell us his motive but would ask us to explain instead."

"Why didn't you tell me this earlier?" said Yao-shan. "Your description has given me the chance to meet Brother Huai-hai today."

T'an-sheng became enlightened in the course of the conversation.

Sometimes it may take many years and great effort to know a person or to understand something. Twenty years are not sufficient, and three thousand miles may not seem like a great distance either. Pai-chang Huai-hai was not known until there was nothing else to be said about him. This is what is meant by "a sentence that contains all the flavors."

Soldiers of the Country

Once, while a regiment was out conducting strategic training, some officers decided that the temple of Ch'an Master Êrh-shan was the best place for cover and concealment of the troops. After settling in, the officers asked the monastics of the monastery to provide them with three meals per day.

Êrh-shan instructed the cook, "Serve them the same food we eat."

The soldiers were very much annoyed with the food they were served because they were not used to eating just green vegetables and radishes, without any fish or meat. An officer went to Master Êrh-shan and reproached him, "Who do you think we are?"

"I think that we are all a part of the same family," said the Master.

"How can you serve us simple food such as boiled vegetables and radishes?" inquired the officer.

The Master politely explained, "Since the green vegetables and radishes are everyday food, one will not become bored with them."

The officer became even more enraged. Again he shouted, "We're the soldiers of the country. We don't hesitate to sacrifice our lives in the struggle against our enemies!"

Êrh-shan's response was equally impolite as he shouted in a loud voice, "We're the envoys of the Dharma on Earth. We've given up everything to save all beings!"

The clergies of various religions have made and continue to make invaluable contributions toward world peace and the happiness of humankind. Violence, natural and humanly-produced calamities, terrorism, and the threat of war exist in the world. People are in a constant state of anxiety. They feel that they are living in the shadow of death. Without religion to reassure the public, society would be even more chaotic.

The *Sangha* has given up material possessions and family ties to transmit the Dharma and enable people to find spiritual sustenance. To be willing to devote one's life to others and live simply are not tasks that everyone can accomplish. For as the old saying goes: "Leading a monastic life is a course for great beings, even a courageous general might not be able to assume such a life."

Chanting Without Sound

One day, Hao-yüeh asked Chao-chou, "What is *Dhāranī?*"[40]

Chao-chou did not say a word, but he merely gestured toward the right side of his meditation mat.

"This?" asked Hao-yüeh, unconvinced.

"Why not?" inquired Chao-chou, "The monastics chant it."

"What else can they chant?" inquired Hao-yüeh.

The Master then gestured toward the left side of the mat.

Hao-yüeh asked incredulously, "That?"

"Why not?" retorted Chao-chou, "The monastics can chant it too."

"Why don't I hear them chanting it?" asked Hao-yüeh.

Chao-chou explained, "Don't you know real chanting doesn't make any sound, and real listening doesn't involve hearing?"

"Do you mean sound and hearing don't enter the Dharma-realm?" asked Hao-yüeh.

"No." Chao-chou replied, "If one departs from the visible in order to see, one can't have true vision, and if one departs from the audible in order to hear, it is false hearing."

"Could you elaborate on your statement that true vision and hearing are not separated from the visible and the audible?" inquired Hao-yüeh.

Master Chao-chou explained in a verse:

> Whatever we see is not form,
> Nor is whatever we hear sound.
> Our eyes are always in contact with Mañjuśrī,
> Our ears always hear the sound of Kuan-yin.
> When we integrate the three elements of body,
>   speech, and mind into one,
> And attain true equality with the four stages of
>   origination, duration, degeneration, and
>   dissolution,
> We will truly understand that there is no
>   distinction between the Buddha and human
>   beings,
> Within the true nature of the Dharma-realm.

Average people hope to become a Buddha immediately. Thus, they often turn to esoteric incantations and teachings. Like Hao-yüeh, they do not understand that form, including the sound of preaching, does not have any true nature to be grasped, and thus, is empty. Although Chao-chou explained to him that esoteric incantations were nothing but form and therefore were empty, Hao-yüeh

mistook him to mean that sound and preaching could not enter the Dharma-realm. He did not know that the Dharma-realm manifested itself without excluding form. Thus, "existing on Earth, the Dharma does not withdraw from what is worldly. Departing from worldly truth or common principles while attempting to attain enlightenment is like searching for a rabbit's horn."

Better Nothing than Something Good

Once, Ch'an Master Chao-chou recited a Ch'an phrase, "The Buddha is 'worry,' and 'worry' is the Buddha."

The novice monks who were present failed to perceive the meaning and asked, "About whom is the Buddha worrying?"

"All sentient beings!" exclaimed Chao-chou.

"But how can the Buddha be relieved of his worries?" inquired a novice.

"Why should he do that?" retorted Chao-chou gravely.

Another time, Master Chao-chou saw his disciple, Wen-yen, making prostrations to the Buddha. He struck him with his staff and asked, "What are you doing?"

"Making prostrations to the Buddha!" declared Wen-yen.

"Is the Buddha here just for us to make prostrations?" Chao-chou asked.

"Making a prostration is at least doing something good," argued Wen-yen.

"Doing something good is not necessarily as good as engaging in non-activity," Chao-chou countered.

Worries as well as the Buddha's Path are diseases. Do Buddhas and bodhisattvas really have diseases? Of course not! They suffer on behalf of all sentient beings. Thus, the Buddha was born on Earth to transform this place of good and evil, in which all beings are subject to transmigration. Kuan-yin became submerged in the ocean of suffering to transform it. Ti-tsang is determined to forgo becoming a Buddha until all sentient beings have been saved from hell. Therefore, why should the Buddha and bodhisattvas be liberated from the worries and grievances for sentient beings?

Although prostrating to the Buddha is considered a pious act, one should not remain attached to such attempts to acquire merit. The real "good" consists of not being fixated on one's activities.

Not Knowing the *Dharmakāya*

Once, Abbot Fu from T'ai-yuan was expounding the *Nirvana Sutra* at Kuang-hsiao Temple in Yangchou. While he was explaining the *Dharmakāya* and the profundity of its essence, a monk in the audience suddenly burst into laughter. After the Abbot finished his lecture, he invited the monk to have tea with him.

During the conversation, the Abbot said, "I explained Buddhism according to the sutras. I know my understanding of the Buddha's teaching is still shallow, and this made you laugh. Please be compassionate and provide me with some suggestions."

The monk said, "Abbot Fu, you were trying to elucidate the *Dharmakāya* just now, but I don't think that you truly understand it."

"Could you be more specific?" inquired the Abbot.

"Please repeat what you said in the lecture," the monk requested.

"All right. The truth of the *Dharmakāya* is like the universe. Vertically, it covers the past, the present, and the future, while horizontally, it encompasses the ten directions. It fills the gap between heaven and Earth. It is all-pervasive and responds to all appeals and circumstances."

The monk then said, "There is nothing wrong with what you have said, but you don't know the wondrous use of the *Dharmakāya*."

"Please be compassionate and tell me," Abbot Fu implored.

"Do you trust me?" asked the monk.

"Why shouldn't I?"

"All right." The monk instructed, "Stop lecturing on the sutras for ten days. Detach your mind from all ideas and intentions, good or evil. Just sit and meditate!"

Abbot Fu did as he was instructed. He stayed up and sat in meditation until dawn each day. One day, he heard drumbeats and horns blowing. Suddenly, he understood what the monk meant and knocked on his door.

The monk came out and said, "I told you to uphold the great Dharma. Why do you behave like a drunkard in the middle of the night?"

Abbot Fu replied, "I've just realized that when I expounded the sutras before, I paid too much attention to the meaning of the words. I wasn't free and liberated; it was as if I were tightly pinching my parents' noses. From now on, I'll never flaunt my knowledge of the sutras."

After that, Abbot Fu stopped giving lectures and traveled far and wide, and he eventually became famous.

The *Dharmakāya* is the Truth, our true nature. The patriarchs expounded the essence of the Truth. Their teachings of "*nirvana*," "*bhūtatathatā*," "fundamental reality," "*prajñā*," "*tathāgatagarbha*," and "the way of non-duality" are components of the *Dharmakāya*. The *Dharmakāya* is not accessible to rational understanding. Its universal nature has to be realized through personal experience; a little more of the *Dharmakāya* is realized when a little more ignorance is overcome.

Our Way of Ch'an

A novice monk once called on Ch'an Master Yüeh-hsi and asked, "Master, I have studied Buddhism and Confucianism for twenty years; but I'm still utterly ignorant of the way of Ch'an. Could you please teach me?"

The Master did not say a word in reply. Instead, he slapped the monk on the face. The novice was astonished and immediately sped out of the meditation hall. He then thought: "This master is strange. I'll go back and argue with him." Just then, he ran into the senior head monk.

The monk kindly asked, "What happened? Come and have a cup of tea with me. Nothing should anger a Ch'an practitioner."

While they were having tea, the novice complained that Ch'an Master Yüeh-hsi slapped him without provocation. Unexpectedly, the head monk also slapped him. The cup dropped from the monk's hand,

and it shattered. Then the senior monk said, "You claimed that you knew Buddhism and Confucianism, and you only needed to know the way of Ch'an. I have just offered it to you. Do you understand?"

The novice was dumbfounded.

The Master asked him again if he understood, but he still did not know what to say. The monk continued, "Excuse me, but let me show you our way of Ch'an!" As he said this, he picked up the broken pieces of the teacup and then wiped the floor with a rag. When he finished, he said, "Besides this, no other way of Ch'an exists."

The novice finally realized that Ch'an was around him. From that time on, he became a disciple of Master Yüeh-hsi.

In the Ch'an School, instruction often includes beating and scolding the student. Although this appears inconsistent with the gentleness, detachment, and composure that we normally associate with Ch'an Buddhists, it has been claimed that these methods are legitimate aspects of Ch'an. The intent is to demonstrate that the way of Ch'an is swift and forceful, that it could be felt within one's flesh and bones. A Ch'an master is flexible enough either to stand up straight or to bend over. As demonstrated, he is able to strike a teacup from someone's hand or pick up the broken pieces and mop the floor. Is this not sufficient to stimulate comprehension?

Confessing for Oneself and for Others

Once, a devotee asked Master P'u-chiao, "If I practice by the Buddha's methods of confession and repentance, for whom should I confess, for myself or for others? If I do it for myself, from where does my evil nature come? Also, how can I confess for others, since I am not they?"

The Master did not know how to answer the questions. So he began to travel and visit other masters to find the answer. One day, he went to Ch'an Master Le-t'an. He had just entered the room when Le-t'an shouted loudly, "Ah!"

P'u-chiao did not understand what this meant, but since he had come to seek for the Buddhist teaching, he was still prepared to pose his question. Before he could even utter a word, Master Le-t'an hit him with his monk's staff. P'u-chiao did not have any idea what this was all about, so he restrained himself and kept silent.

A few days later, P'u-chiao was back in Le-t'an's room. Le-t'an told him, "I would like to discuss an ancient *kung-an* with you."

Before P'u-chiao had time to give his assent, Le-t'an let out another "Ah!"

P'u-chiao suddenly became enlightened and could not help laughing. Master Le-t'an came down from his meditation mat and held P'u-chiao's hand, saying, "Do you know the Dharma?"

P'u-chiao exclaimed, "Ah!" and he pushed Le-t'an's hand away, whereupon the latter burst into laughter.

The methods of confession and repentance vary in degree. For example, there are confession and repentance concerning deeds, merit, immortality, and so on. According to the Buddhist sutras: "Since evil comes from the [illusory] mind, the [illusory] mind should be eliminated. When this is done, evil will be completely eliminated as well. The type of confession in which both the evil and its source, the [illusory] mind, are eradicated can be called a true one." Moreover, when one confesses for oneself, one simultaneously does it for others. The opposite is also true. This is because self and others are one, and the fundamental principle underlying phenomenal activities is absolute. Therefore, why should we attempt to seclude ourselves from other beings?

Conventionally, there are wrong doings, and retribution will accompany them as a result. However, there are no such things as wrong doings and retribution that exist in the true nature. Is the exclamation "Ah!" good or evil, permanent or temporary, self or other? In an absolute sense, beings do not differ from one another.

Incense Merits

Prime Minister P'ei-hsiu of the T'ang dynasty was a devout Buddhist. His son, P'ei Wen-tê, finished first in the most prestigious imperial examination and became the highest ranked scholar at an early age. Therefore, the emperor made him a member of the Imperial Academy.

However, P'ei-hsiu did not want his son to experience a meteoric rise so early in life, only to burn out just as quickly. Therefore, he sent him to a temple to study and practice Buddhism. There, the young man was asked to perform manual labor, such as tending the kitchen fire and fetching water. Such drudgery left the successful young scholar exhausted every day. He became very annoyed and developed a grudge against his father for sending him there to be a beast of burden. Nonetheless, he could not disobey his father's order.

After enduring the hard labor grudgingly for some time, he could no longer restrain himself from complaining bitterly, "A scholar of the Imperial Academy streams with sweat from carrying water in the temple. How can monks bear it, if they dare to drink it?"

The Abbot, Ch'an Master Wu-tê, happened to hear his complaint. With a smile, he answered by reciting the following: "Even by burning just one stick of incense, this old monk can digest an immeasurable amount of grain."

P'ei Wen-tê was appalled. From that time forward, he concentrated on meditation and manual labor.

A great person does not only live to be venerated by others. By performing manual labor, Ch'an practitioners are tested of their will power and their practice of Buddhism. Confucianism holds: "Before heaven entrusts people with important tasks, their will power must be tested, their bones and muscles fatigued, and their body starved." Buddhism advocates even more strongly the necessity of a simple life and manual labor. However, these are only worldly endeavors resulting in merits and blessings. While a Ch'an practitioner's mind can cover ten directions of space horizontally, one's Buddha-nature can cover the past, present, and future vertically. This simply implies that the practitioner had attained the supramundane state of mind; hence, "burning one stick of incense, this old monk can digest an immeasurable amount of grain."

Awaiting Rescue

There once was a devout lay Buddhist. One day, he was caught in a flood and had to take refuge on the roof of a house. The floodwater was rising steadily. Soon, the water was above his ankles. He hastily prayed, "Kuan-yin! Kuan-yin! Please come and rescue me immediately!"

Not before long, an aborigine came in a canoe who offered to rescue him. He refused by saying, "I don't want your help. I'll have Kuan-yin save me." Having been rebuffed, the aborigine rowed away.

The floodwater steadily rose up to the waist of the Buddhist. Hence, he prayed impatiently, "Bodhisattva, please come soon!" A motorboat pulled up, and the people in it offered to take him to safety. Again he refused, saying, "Throughout my life, I've disdained scientific technology. I hate anything that is mechanical. The Bodhisattva will save me." So the people in the motorboat sped away.

Now the water was up to his chest and he cried out, "Come and rescue me immediately, Kuan-yin!" A moment later, a helicopter arrived which was piloted by a foreigner. The Buddhist refused his help, exclaiming, "I don't want your help. Kuan-yin will save me."

The man was about to drown. Fortunately, Ch'an Master Fo-kuang happened to pass by and rescued him. The Buddhist complained, "I'm such a devout Buddhist. Why didn't Kuan-yin come to rescue me?"

Master Fo-kuang replied, "It's unfair of you to say that. When the floodwater was up to your ankles, Kuan-yin came to rescue you in the canoe, but you spurned the man paddling it because he was an aborigine. Kuan-yin had no other alternatives but to use a motorboat to save you. Yet you resented scientific technology and refused again. Finally, Kuan-yin used a helicopter, but you rejected it due to the foreign pilot. The Bodhisattva tried time and time again to save you. Not only were you ungrateful to her, but you continued to complain. I really shouldn't have bothered to save you. I should have let you check in at the Palace of Hell."

Kuan-yin has thirty-three manifestations. If one only has faith, and lack the wisdom of Ch'an, one cannot realize that "the fresh green bamboos are nothing but the manifestations of the Buddha's body, while the blooming yellow flowers are the embodiment of wisdom."

Perfect Meditation

Once, as the Buddha was expounding the Dharma, a woman beside him entered into *samādhi*. Having seen this, Mañjuśrī asked, "Buddha! How can this woman sit beside you and enter into *samādhi*? Why can't I do the same, despite my reputation for being the wisest?"

"You had better bring her out of her *samādhi* and ask her yourself," replied the Buddha.

Mañjuśrī attempted to follow the Buddha's suggestion. First, he walked around her three times, then he snapped his fingers. He even lifted her to the heavens. Although he exhausted all his supernatural powers, she remained undisturbed.

The Buddha said to him, "Even if there were thousands of manifestations of you present, you still could not bring her out of *samādhi*. If you insist on doing so, you had better invite Avidyā to come and help."

Avidyā appeared, prostrated to the Buddha, and went up to the woman. With one snap of his fingers, she was aroused from *samādhi*.

Avidyā means ignorance and illusion. Normally, when one is in *samādhi*, one cannot be disturbed even if someone as omnipotent as Mañjuśrī tries. Whereas the wisdom of Mañjuśrī could not disturb the woman, ignorance could. The effects of defilements caused by ignorance and illusion cannot be overlooked. Someone's casual remarks may please you or upset you, or an unexpected incident may make you happy or angry.

Without the composure possible through Ch'an meditation, life would be very difficult. If anyone wants us to rejoice, one only has to flatter us and we will become overjoyed. On the other hand, if someone wants to annoy us, any vicious remarks will serve the purpose. If others can control our moods to this extent, it means that we need to meditate more. The woman was a good example. She was not distracted by Mañjuśrī, but when Avidyā arrived, all her resistance was destroyed.

Drawing Pictures of Cakes

After Ch'an Master Pai-chang passed away, Hsiang-yen Chih-hsien went to join Ch'an Master Kuei-shan Ling-yu. When they met, Kuei-shan asked, "I heard that when you were with the late Master Pai-chang you could answer any question after only being given a few hints. Those were simply questions and answers concerning intellectual knowledge. What I would like for you to demonstrate now is not the knowledge that you have acquired through your life experiences or what is recorded in the sutras. I want you to tell me what your obligation was before you were born. Then, I will tell you if you are right."

Hsiang-yen was dumbfounded and did not know how to reply. After pondering for a while, he said, "Please tell me the answer."

Kuei-shan said, "But whatever I say is merely my opinion. What good will it do you?"

Hsiang-yen then went to the preaching hall. He thumbed through all the sutras but did not come across the appropriate answer to the question. He sighed, "Talking about food can't make one full, nor can one allay one's hunger by drawing pictures of cakes." So saying, he committed all his Buddhist texts to flames and swore, "I will never study any more doctrines. It's just a waste of time. I'll simply be an alms-begging monk."

Hsiang-yen then bade farewell to Master Kuei-shan and went to Nanyang. He lived in the same place where the Imperial Preceptor Hui-chung had lived and practiced in solitude.

One day, while he was weeding, his hoe accidentally hit a tile. When he heard the clanging sound, he became enlightened and chanted:

> With one timely blow, all acquired knowledge
>   are forgotten,
> There is no need to rely upon cultivation.
> The ancient path can be propagated through
>   one's actions and gestures,
> Without attachment to the teachings,
> Which is nowhere to be found.
> One's demeanor is beyond sound and form.
> All those who have attained the Path
>   teach the highest form of non-attachment.

This kung-an demonstrates that knowledge and being awakened to the Truth are two different matters. While the former is acquired through differentiation, the latter is realized through the understanding of the equality of all things. The realization of Ch'an cannot be attained simply by sitting in meditation. It requires progression from knowledge based on discrimination to the wisdom of non-discrimination. Therefore, had Hsiang-yen not acquired the wisdom necessary to explain all things, he could not have attained realization, even if he had broken the tile with an iron hammer.

Ch'an Is Not an Object

Once, Master Shih-t'ou asked Master Pao-t'ung, "Are you a ts'an Ch'an (Ch'an practicing) monk or a roving monk?"

"I'm a ts'an Ch'an monk," replied Pao-t'ung.

"What is Ch'an?" Shih-t'ou asked.

"Lifting the eyebrows and blinking the eyes," declared Pao-t'ung.

"Put these aside and show me your true face."

"I would like to ask you to put these aside," Pao-t'ung retorted.

"I don't judge you by the way you lift your eyebrows and blink your eyes," said Shih-t'ou.

"I've already presented Ch'an to you!" exclaimed Pao-t'ung.

"Besides the lifting of the eyebrows and the blinking of the eyes, are there any differences between our minds?" queried Shih-t'ou.

"They're not different from the mind of Ch'an," replied Pao-t'ung.

"These are matters that don't concern us," said Shih-t'ou.

"It is precisely these matters that do concern us."

"Ch'an is not an object!" Shih-t'ou declared.

"But every object is Ch'an," added Pao-t'ung.

Finally, Master Shih-t'ou stated, "Real Ch'an isn't an object, nor can any object be grasped. From what you have said, I think your understanding needs more cultivation."

Ch'an is vivacious. In meditation, if one can realize that all things are empty, one will be able to recognize in daily life "the fresh green bamboos are nothing but the *dharmakāya*, while the blooming yellow flowers are all *prajñā*." Actions such as walking, standing, sitting, and reclining are Ch'an. Lifting one's eyebrows and blinking one's eyes are also Ch'an. If one can understand this tacitly, then there is no need to express it in language. Pao-t'ung could not withstand Master Shih-t'ou's incisive questioning and said that every object is Ch'an. The *Diamond Sutra* states: "The Dharma revealed by the *Tathāgata* cannot be grasped or spoken because it does not exist (it is empty by nature), nor does it not exist (it is not attached to the emptiness)." Hence, Shih-t'ou advised Pao-t'ung to exert a greater effort in meditation.

The Rooster and the Bug

A seven-year-old boy often went to see Ch'an Master Wu-tê. Since the boy was very loquacious, the Master gradually discovered that he was quick-witted and had potential for Ch'an. One day, Wu-tê said to him, "I'm very busy. I don't have time to argue and talk nonsense with you. I'll give you one more chance to debate with me. If you lose, you'll have to treat me to some cake. If I lose, I'll buy some cake for you."

Upon hearing this, the boy replied, "Please take out your money, Master!"

"But the loser will take out his money. Now, let's begin. I'll pretend to be a rooster."

"I'll pretend to be a bug," said the boy.

Wu-tê seized this opportunity and said immediately, "A little bug! Well, you should buy cakes for this big rooster."

But the boy would not give up so easily. He argued, "No, Master! You'll have to buy them for me because I'll fly away whenever I see you. This is proper because a master and a disciple aren't supposed to debate with each other. In that sense, haven't you lost?"

Holding the lad's hand, Wu-tê went around and gathered together many villagers, saying, "As with questions of war or peace that government officials cannot decide, we'll have to leave it up to the villagers. Our present situation is similar to that. Since there are three hundred of you here, please judge for us who is right." He then repeated the debate, but the villagers could not decide. Having seen this,

Master Wu-tê said seriously and solemnly, "Only Ch'an masters who have their eyes wide open can decide."

Three days later, people in the monastery noticed that Wu-tê quietly bought some cake for the boy.

What a rooster and what a bug! Many humorous episodes must have taken place between these two Ch'an practitioners, despite the great difference in their ages.

In Ch'an, large or small, long or short, right or wrong, and good or bad do not exist, nor are there winners or losers. Initially, Master Wu-tê wanted to win, so he pretended to be a big, strong rooster. The seven-year-old boy was willing to be a small, weak insect that could be easily pecked at by the rooster. Yet, the insect could fly away, implying that a master and a disciple should not argue with each other. This illustrates that Ch'an eschews debates, although it does have its own standards of etiquette.

Acquiring Charm

There once was a lady almsgiver who was very rich. Few could match her in wealth, social status, power, competence, or beauty. Nonetheless, she constantly felt depressed. One day, she went to Master Wu-tê, wanting to know how to acquire charm so that others would like her.

Wu-tê told her, "You will charm others if you can cooperate with different people under all circumstances and at all times. Furthermore, if you have a compassionate heart like the Buddha's, you will speak words of Ch'an, listen to the sound of Ch'an, carry out the work of Ch'an, and have the mind of Ch'an."

"What are the words of Ch'an?" asked the woman.

"They are happy, factual, and modest words, which benefit others."

"What should I do to hear the sound of Ch'an?" she inquired.

"You must transform all sounds into refined ones. That is, you must be able to turn insults hurled at you into compassionate sounds and transform slander into encouragement. When you no longer take offense at the sound of others weeping or clamoring, at harsh or unpleasant noises, you will be able to hear the sound of Ch'an."

The woman continued, "What is the work of Ch'an?"

Wu-tê replied, "It refers to almsgiving, charity, service to others, and all actions that conform to the Dharma."

Finally, she implored, "What is the mind of Ch'an?"

"It is the harmony between your mind and mine and the minds of saints and average people which bless all beings."

Soon, the woman abandoned her arrogant manner, refrained from flaunting her wealth, and stopped capitalizing on her beauty. She became modest and courteous. She was also polite to others and solicitous toward her family members. In a short duration, people praised her as "the most charming almsgiver."

Ch'an is not a theory, but rather, it is life. When Ch'an is implemented into daily life, people will respect and dwell in harmony with each other. Ch'an will help people succeed in their pursuits.

Not Losing One's Bearings

The first time Ch'an Master Hsien-ju, who was from Lo-fu Shan, visited Ch'an Master Ching-hsüan in Ta-yang Shan, Hupei, the latter asked him, "Where do you live?"

"I live in I-shan," answered Hsien-ju.

"How far is it from here?" Ching-hsüan asked.

Hsien-ju replied, "Five thousand miles."

"How did you get here? Did you walk?" inquired Ching-hsüan.

"No, I didn't," Hsien-ju replied.

"Can you fly?" Ching-hsüan asked.

"No, I can't," said Hsien-ju.

"Then, how did you get here?" Ching-hsüan repeated.

Hsien-ju replied, "By not losing my bearings and by remaining inconspicuous."

Ching-hsüan asked, "Have you already transcended *samādhi*?"

"If the mind of the Buddha cannot be grasped, how can *samādhi* manifest itself?" observed Hsien-ju.

Ching-hsüan agreed, "That is so, that is so. With your belief, you can see the one reality. Please take care."

Ching-hsüan was a Ch'an master of great attainment during the Sung dynasty. He became a monk with his uncle, Chih-t'ung. When he became fully ordained at the age of nineteen, Ching-hsüan already demonstrated a great understanding of Ch'an. For example, when he attended a lecture on perfect enlightenment, he asked why it was named perfect enlightenment. While visiting Ch'an Master Yüan-kuan's monastery, he asked what such a monastery without form would be like. His Ch'an power was exhibited through his wide-ranging inquisitiveness. Whenever he saw clergies who were dying, he would inquire about their destination. If he came across clergies who were growing melons, he asked when they would be ripe. However, when other practitioners asked him questions, he always replied with a verse. He was a Ch'an master of unusual literary talent as well.

Hsien-ju traveled from Szechuan to visit Ching-hsüan. His claim to have walked a long distance without stepping on the ground indicates that there is no time, space, or distance in Ch'an. The fact that he did not lose his bearings showed that Ching-hsüan and he were destined to meet. Later, Hsien-ju became enlightened while studying with Ching-hsüan.

The Path of Perfect Harmony

Ch'an Master Yao-shan told Ch'an Master Shih-t'ou Hsi-ch'ien, "I know something about the scriptures and the twelve divisions of the Mahayana canon. Still I have never been able to understand why people in the South say that by 'directly pointing to one's mind, and seeing one's [true] nature, one will become a Buddha.' I earnestly request your instruction."

Shih-t'ou said, "Neither is affirmation nor negation correct, nor is it correct to negate what is affirmed or to affirm what is negated. What shall we do?"

Yao-shan began to understand but not quite thoroughly. Shih-t'ou said, "You don't belong here. You had better go to Master Ma-tsu."

When Yao-shan met Ma-tsu, he repeated the same question that he had asked Shih-t'ou. Ma-tsu replied, "Sometimes I call it 'lifting the eyebrows and blinking the eyes.' But sometimes I don't call it that. Sometimes 'lifting the eyebrows and blinking the eyes' is the answer. Sometimes, it isn't. How can you recognize this?"

Upon hearing this, Yao-shan made a prostration to Ma-tsu without saying a word. The latter asked, "What have you realized? Why did you prostrate to me?"

Yao-shan answered, "Now I understand that when I was with Master Shih-t'ou, I was just like a mosquito trying to bite an iron ox."

Understanding a concept means achieving mastery through comprehensive study until one has grasped it clearly. Practicing what one has seen and understood is a matter of spirituality. How well one does this cannot be described in detail. As in the example of drinking water, only the one who drinks knows whether it is cold or hot.

Yao-shan traveled between "Kiangsi and Hunan," from Ch'an Master Shih-t'ou in Hunan to Ma-tsu in Kiangsi, in search of the Truth. Shih-t'ou told him to put aside affirmation and negation, while Ma-tsu said that lifting the eyebrows and blinking the eyes simultaneously are and are not the same thing. Actually, affirmation and negation share the same eternal, impersonal, and unchangeable reality, as do emptiness and non-emptiness. The essence of Ch'an is the Path of perfect harmony.

Picking Up Leaves

Ch'an Master Ting-chou was walking in the courtyard with a novice monk. Suddenly, a gust of wind blew many leaves off a tree. The Master bent over to pick them up and put them in his pockets.

The novice said to him, "Master! You don't have to do that. We'll sweep the courtyard tomorrow morning."

The Master objected to his suggestion, "You shouldn't say that. Will sweeping definitely make the yard cleaner? If I pick up one leaf, there will be one less on the ground. It will be cleaner than if I don't do it."

"But, Master!" protested the novice, "There are so many leaves that are falling. The moment you pick one up, another may fall on the same spot. How will you be able to finish the task?"

Ting-chou replied as he continued picking up leaves, "Leaves don't just fall on the ground, but they also fall in our minds. I am picking up those that are in my mind. Eventually, I'll clean up all of them."

Upon hearing this, the novice began to understand the purpose of the life of Ch'an practitioners.

When the Buddha was alive, he had a disciple who was not very bright. This disciple was so dull that every time he memorized a new verse during chanting, he would forget the one he had previously learned. The Buddha had no alternative but to find another method, so he asked him what he was good at doing. The disciple replied that he knew how to sweep the floor. The Buddha told him to chant "whisk off the dust and clean up the trash" while he was working. After some time, the disciple began to think: "If one uses a broom to sweep away rubbish, what should one do to wipe off the dust in one's mind?" Consequently, he became wise and eventually attained enlightenment.

By picking up leaves, Ting-chou was actually eradicating erroneous thoughts and worries from his own mind. It does not matter how many fallen leaves there are on Earth. As for those in our minds, it decreases the sum total by one, when we pick one up. As Buddhists, when we have attained a peace of mind, we possess all phenomena. Confucian scholars hold that in order to achieve anything, individuals should start with their own self-cultivation. Ch'an practitioners believe that a pure mind will automatically bring forth the Pure Land, and we should continue to pick up our fallen leaves.

Using the Sutras for Toilet Paper!?

One of Ch'an Master Pai-yin's disciples believed that he was already enlightened. Thus, he did not pay homage to the Buddha in any way. Worse still, he used pages torn from the scriptures of the *Mahāprajñā-pāramitā Sutra* for toilet paper. He often boasted, "I'm a Buddha. Now that I have a Buddha here within me, these sutras have become useless. Why shouldn't I use them as toilet paper?"

When Ch'an Master Pai-yin heard this, he told the disciple, "I've been told that you are a Buddha now. Congratulations! But don't you think a Buddha's bottom is too noble to be cleansed by such trash? I suggest you use better quality toilet paper."

Some Ch'an practitioners think that awakening to the Truth means acting in a bizarre manner. Actually, they should not scold the Buddha or curse the patriarchs as they please. Using the Buddhist sutras for toilet paper may be acceptable, but only after one completely understands the Buddhist teaching and the universal Dharma. Otherwise, both good quality paper and poor quality paper should be used wisely, to avoid wasting paper.

The Master Becomes the Son-in-Law

Ch'an Master I-hsiu had such an enlightened mind that he could reverse the course of events simply by chatting and laughing.

One day, a devotee implored him, "Master! I don't want to live any more. I want to commit suicide."

I-hsiu asked, "Everything seems to be going fine with you. Why are you thinking about suicide?"

The man explained, "Oh, Master! Since my business went bankrupt, my debts are up to my ears. My creditors leave me no way out except death."

"Are you sure there's no other way out?" asked I-hsiu.

"Yes. Except for my little daughter, I don't have anything else to my name," replied the devotee sadly.

Upon hearing this, I-hsiu had a sudden inspiration. "Ah! I have a solution. Why don't you find a good man to marry your daughter and then ask him to help you pay the debts?"

The man answered dejectedly, "But my daughter is only eight years old. How can she get married?"

I-hsiu said, "You can marry your daughter to me. Let me be your son-in-law and help you with the debts."

The devotee was startled and turned pale. "You must be joking. You're my master. How can you be my son-in-law?"

I-hsiu seemed to have a well thought out plan. He gestured to the man to be quiet. "I want to help you. It's settled. Go and announce the marriage immediately. Remember, on the wedding day, I'll go to your house as your son-in-law. Leave now and make preparations."

This man had always believed in Master I-hsiu's wisdom, so he immediately made it known that on a certain day the Master would go to his home as his son-in-law. The news was widely circulated and made a stir in town. On the wedding day, the man's house was packed with curious bystanders. When Master I-hsiu arrived, he told the man to put a table in front of the door. Also, the man was to place a writing brush, ink, and paper on the table. In a short while, the Master began to write calligraphy. Seeing that I-hsiu's work was very good, the guests vied with each other to purchase samples. They completely forgot why they were there. The sales went so well that in the end, the money accumulated filled several large baskets.

Pointing at the money, I-hsiu asked the man, "Is this enough for you to pay for your debts?"

Nodding happily, the man replied, "It's enough. It's enough. Master, you're really infinitely resourceful to have made so much money."

"All right. Now that the problem is solved, I'm not your son-in-law any more. Let me continue to be your master. Goodbye."

People who practice and know how to use Ch'an wisely can solve problems easily.

Who Is the Ch'an Master?

When meditating, Ch'an Master Fo-kuang often forgot about himself." Sometimes his attendants informed him that a particular monk or novice from a certain province was waiting outside to pay his respects and request instructions. At that point, Fo-kuang always asked, "But who is the Ch'an master whom he wants to see?"

Sometimes, while he was having a meal, his attendants would ask him, "Master, are you full?"

Perplexed, he would ask in reply, "Who has eaten?"

One day, the Master weeded the fields from morning until night without any rest. Later, when the monastics in the monastery saw him, they all said admiringly, "Master, you have been working really hard."

He inquired politely, "Who has worked hard?"

"Who has eaten?" "Who is speaking?" "Who has worked hard?" Ch'an Master Fo-kuang often would respond to a question with questions like these. Many Ch'an practitioners found and understood themselves through such answers.

People in this world sometimes overemphasize their own thoughts, knowledge, and possessions. By doing so, they lose themselves. On other occasions, they deny everything. They thus confuse themselves and subsequently lose their grounding and become utterly worthless. However, once they have acquired Ch'an, they actually possess everything, even when they deny it. They can also liberate themselves even when they affirm everything. Hence, a Ch'an Buddhist's speech, silence, and movement possess much deeper implications. Their everyday activities and repose have special meaning. Although their words and deeds may seem simple and dull to some people, they are actually profound and have many wonderful flavors. Though their verbal exchanges may sound severe, they are philosophical and can provide people with congenial guidance. Henceforth, Fo-kuang demonstrated that he was one of them by asking the question "Who is the Ch'an Master?"

A Beggar and Ch'an

T'iao-shui, who was very well-versed in Ch'an, had taught in many places.

While T'iao-shui was the abbot at a monastery, he attracted many novices. However, most of these novices could not bear the hardships or tolerate the arduous work, hence they gave up searching for the Dharma halfway through. This situation left him with no other choice but to resign his position. He told the novices to leave and go their own ways, and he disappeared afterwards.

Three years later, one of his disciples found T'iao-shui living with a group of beggars under a bridge in the capital. He immediately implored the Master to instruct him.

T'iao-shui told him curtly, "You're not qualified to receive my instruction."

"How can I become qualified?" asked the disciple.

The Master answered, "If you can live under the bridge like me for a few days, I may be able to help you."

So, the disciple dressed as a beggar and stayed with T'iao-shui that night. The next day, one of the beggars died. At midnight, T'iao-shui and his disciple carried the dead man to the foot of a mountain and buried him. Afterward, they went back to their home under the bridge.

Master T'iao-shui fell asleep immediately, but his disciple remained awake until dawn. When they got up in the morning, T'iao-shui told his student, "We don't need to go out begging today because the dead man has left some food." After seeing the dirty bowl, the disciple could not take even a single bite.

The Master said to him bluntly, "I've told you that you can't study with me. Since you can't enjoy the Pure Land here, you had better go back to your world. Please don't tell anyone where I live. People living in this Pure Land don't want to be disturbed!"

With tears in his eyes, the disciple knelt down and said, "Oh, Master! Please take good care of yourself. I'm really not qualified to be your student because I can't appreciate your Pure Land."

Where is the Pure Land for a Ch'an practitioner? It is in performing lowly tasks. It is in the love for and salvation of others. It is also in the transformation of one's surroundings. Simply stated, the Pure Land is within us and is not found outside of our minds.

Teaching through Skillful Means

Ch'an Master Yang-shan from Canton lived with Kuei-shan in Fuchou for fifteen years and eventually attained realization. After learning the intuitive method of the Ch'an School from Kuei-shan, Yang-shan took the lead in widely proclaiming Buddhism when he was only thirty-five. Thus, he was praised as "little Śākyamuni Buddha."

One day, he stopped a novice monk who was passing by and asked, "From where do you come?"

"The south," answered the novice.

Raising his walking staff and gesturing, the Master queried, "Are the elders of the monasteries there still talking about this?"

"No, they aren't," the novice replied.

Yang-shan continued, "Then, are they still talking about that?"

The novice shook his head again and said, "No."

"Sir!" the Master cried out compassionately to the student, who was cautiously standing by.

"Yes," the novice answered, with his palms joined together.

"Go to the meditation hall," ordered the Master.

As the novice was about to enter the meditation hall, the Master stopped him by calling out, "Sir!"

The novice turned around.

Yang-shan ordered, "Come back to me!"

The novice did as he was instructed. Yang-shan touched his head with the staff and said, "Go!"

Upon hearing this, the novice finally attained realization.

Yang-shan's method of teaching was appropriate for his student, demonstrating the Master's command of skillful means. Thus, the novice could become enlightened under his instruction. Yang-shan first made it clear to the novice that there was no difference among east, west, north, and south, or between this and that, and he told him to go to the meditation hall. By doing so, he enabled the novice to realize that the Dharma and Ch'an existed everywhere. Afterward, he asked the student to return to him. This indicated that the Path leading to the Dharma was right before him. Finally, when the novice went over to him, Yang-shan told him to leave. This showed that there was no coming or going in the Dharma, because it covered the ten directions of space as well as the three worlds. With this skillful method of teaching, how could the student fail to attain realization?

Competing to Be the Greatest

T'ung-tu Temple in Korea is also called the Buddha's Temple because of its collection of the Buddha's robes. Hai-yin Temple, called the Temple of the Dharma, collected the complete Buddhist Canon which was engraved in wood. While the former had more than 4,000 acres of land, the latter had more than twice that amount.

Monastics from both temples encountered each other while traveling; so they decided to journey together. Once, while resting under a tree, they talked about their respective monasteries and began to argue about which was greater.

Those from T'ung-tu claimed, "Our temple is probably the largest in the country, because of its size and the large number of monastics residing there."

The monastics from the other temple were reluctant to believe them, "What makes you think so?"

One of the former explained, "Because when we serve food, we have to ladle out the soup in a boat."

Not to be outdone, the monastics from Hai-yin Temple countered, "Our temple is bigger. It's the largest in Korea!"

Those from T'ung-tu did not believe them either, "How do you know?"

After thinking for a second, a monk from Hai-yin answered, "When we defecate in our toilet, we have to wait for three minutes before we can hear our excrement reach the bottom of the pit."

It just so happened that a monk who was from Sung-kuang Temple, which is also called the Temple of the *Sangha* (sixteen Ch'an masters from this monastery had served as imperial preceptors for various emperors), was sitting under another tree nearby. He objected to what he had heard, "My temple is the biggest because every monastic there possesses the entire universe within his or her mind. Can any of you top this?"

Which is greater? All Ch'an practitioners talk big because "their minds are like the universe that can embrace as many worlds as the sands of the Ganges." This is the state of mind of a Ch'an practitioner.

Beheading a Snake

A novice monk went to Ch'an Master Chih-ch'ang's temple for instruction. When he arrived, the Master was weeding. Suddenly, a snake slithered out of the thick grass. Without hesitation, Chih-ch'ang cut the snake with his hoe.

The novice did not like what he saw, remarking, "I've always admired your compassionate teaching. But what I have just seen is the behavior of an uncouth layman."

"I wonder who is uncouth, you or me," said the Master.

"What do you mean by uncouth?" the novice retorted.

The Master put down his hoe.

"What does it mean to be cultivated?" the novice persisted.

Master Chih-ch'ang raised his hoe and assumed the stance of killing the snake.

Not knowing what the Master meant, the novice commented, "It's impossible to understand your explanation of what is uncouth or cultivated!"

The Master said, "Let's not talk about being uncouth or cultivated in this way. May I ask where you saw me beheading the snake?"

"Right here," the novice answered impolitely.

Chih-ch'ang rebuked, "Why didn't you see yourself 'right here'? Why did you focus your attention on my killing the snake 'right here'?"

Now the novice began to understand the Master's point.

In the history of the Ch'an School, there is the story of a monk, named Nan-ch'üan, in the T'ang dynasty who killed a cat. Some have blamed him for this act because non-killing is one of the most fundamental precepts of Buddhism. Others have argued that he simply seized a great opportunity to apply Buddhist teachings. Therefore, what he did should not be judged in a narrow context, nor should he be criticized for his actions. Nan-ch'üan's killing the cat simply might be a gesture implying that he wanted to cut off people's persistent attachment to material desires.

Master Chih-ch'ang might have had the same intention when he raised his hoe. The novice responded superficially to the action and accused him of lacking compassion. Master Chih-ch'ang was a noble character who enjoyed high prestige, and he was influential

among his disciples. He told the student not to be preoccupied with what he saw or felt. Since Ch'an tries to eliminate conventional reasoning and common sense knowledge, why should the novice remain attached to the discrimination of phenomena, while neglecting his own self?

Hell

Ch'an Master Wu-tê took in many admiring young novice practitioners who came to study Ch'an with him. He told them to leave everything outside of the monastery. In the meditation hall, he asked the novices to "dedicate their physical bodies to the monasteries and entrust their lives to the Dharma."

Nonetheless, some of the novices were gluttons and sluggards who despised work. Some sought ease and comfort and were interested in secular activities. In an attempt to change their ways, the Master told them the following story:

A man passed away and his soul wandered to another place. When he was about to enter, the door keeper stopped him and asked, "Hey! Do you like to eat? There's plenty of food here. Do you like to sleep? You may sleep here as long as you want without being disturbed. Do you like to enjoy yourself? There are various kinds of recreational activities from which to choose. Do you hate work? You don't need to do anything here. There isn't anyone to discipline you either."

Upon hearing this, the man happily decided to stay. He feasted and then fell asleep. When he woke up, he began to play. While he was having fun, he continued to eat. He did this for three months. Gradually, he began to feel bored. He went to see the door keeper and implored, "Actually, it's no fun to live like this for a very long duration. I've played so much that I've lost interest in any kind of amusement. I've eaten so much that I've put on too much weight. I've slept so much that I've become dull-witted. Could you please give me some work to do?"

"I'm sorry. We don't have any work that needs to be done here."

After another three months had elapsed, the man couldn't tolerate it any more. He told the door keeper, "I can't put up with this kind of life for another day. If you can't find me anything to do, I would rather go to hell."

"You think you've been in heaven?" asked the door keeper in reply. "This is hell. It strips you of all ideals, future prospects, and creativity. It makes you degenerate slowly. Such a torment of the soul is worse than the physical torture of climbing a mountain of swords or being plunged into a pot of boiling oil!"

Practicing Ch'an does not simply mean sitting in meditation with legs crossed and eyes closed, although this is one way to enter Ch'an practice. Ch'an is carrying firewood and water. It is quarrying stones and husking rice with mortar and pestle. It is plowing and weeding. It is tilling the land during the day and studying at night. It also means tolerance and compassion, diligence and sacrifice, skillfulness and flexibility, beatings and scolding. Thus, when you have Ch'an, life is heaven, but it is hell without it.

Where Is the Head Monk?

Ch'an Master Huang-po asked Master Lin-chi to deliver a letter to Master Kuei-shan Ling-yu. Kuei-shan sent Yang-shan to welcome Lin-chi. When Yang-shan received the letter, he remarked, "So, this is a letter from Master Huang-po, the person renowned for his superior wisdom, virtue, and conduct. But, may I ask, where is the letter from the head monk?"

Lin-chi immediately responded, "I've already given it to you."

The two of them then went to see Master Kuei-shan, who asked Lin-chi, "How many monks are there with Master Huang-po?"

"About seven hundred," he replied.

"Who is the head monk?" Kuei-shan asked.

"I've already asked Brother Yang-shan to give you my letter."

Yang-shan took out the letter, "Yes, it's here. I don't know where the head monk is."

Ignoring this remark, Lin-chi addressed Kuei-shan, "May I ask, how many monks do you have here?"

"About 1,500."

"That's a lot," commented Lin-chi.

"Your teacher, Huang-po, also has many," replied Kuei-shan.

Lin-chi inquired, "Since you have so many monks here, could you provide us with a head monk?"

Kuei-shan did not answer the question but instructed Yang-shan to accompany Lin-chi on his return trip. On the way, Yang-shan told Lin-chi, "You had better go north if you want to find a head monk."

"Are you sure?" he asked.

Without hesitation, Yang-shan answered, "Yes. Just go there. Real head monks will acknowledge each other. The only problem is they can't remain together forever."

Lin-chi went north and found Ch'an Master P'u-hua at Chen-chou. When Lin-chi decided to establish a monastery, he asked P'u-hua to serve as its head monk, with himself serving as the assistant. Later, just as Lin-chi's teaching became popular, P'u-hua passed away.

Ch'an masters never reveal their personal or spiritual affairs. Although they are eager to help their students and treat them with compassion, they often conceal their intentions, which can only be understood by intuition.

No One Can Do It for You

A devotee once asked Chao-chou, "Master, how should I meditate in order to be awakened to the Truth?"

Upon hearing this question, Chao-chou immediately stood up and said, "I'm going to urinate." After taking a few steps, he turned around and said to the devotee, "Look. Even such a trifle as urinating has to be taken care of personally. No one else can do it for me."

The Master meant that meditation and the attainment of enlightenment are personal matters. How could the devotee expect anyone else to tell him how to do it? What a lively, brilliant, and penetrating way of teaching!

According to Buddhism, only the one who eats becomes full. Similarly, each person's life and death must be taken care of individually. To become enlightened through meditation, one simply

has to practice it. No one else can do it except oneself, not even one's parents, siblings, or closest friends. From this perspective, each individual must be completely self-reliant in life.

The Three Gates of Buddhism

When Lu Hsi-shêng first visited Ch'an Master Yang-shan, he asked the Master, "If the three gates of the monastery are all open, through which one should I enter?"

"Through the Gate of Faith," answered the Master.

"What good are the other two?" Hsi-shêng asked.

"You may also enter through them," declared the Master.

"What are they?" inquired Hsi-shêng.

"One is the Gate of Wisdom, and the other is the Gate of Compassion," the Master replied.

"If we enter through only one, why do we need three?" Hsi-shêng asked pointedly.

Yang-shan explained, "Those who use the Gate of Faith enter through the Buddha, those who use the Gate of Wisdom enter through the Dharma, and those who use the Gate of Compassion enter through the *Sangha*. In other words, one may enter the Buddha's Path by means of any one of the Gates of the Three Precious Ones."

Inside the preaching hall, Lu Hsi-shêng continued his questioning, "What will happen if one enters the Buddha realm without leaving the realm of the demons?"

Master Yang-shan waved his whisk upside down three times. After seeing this, Lu Hsi-shêng prostrated and then asked, "Master, do you still keep the precepts?"

"No!" he snapped.

"Do you still sit in meditation?"

Again the Master declared, "No!" Lu Hsi-shêng was lost in thought. The Master asked, "Do you understand?"

"No!" he exclaimed.

Yang-shan then explained what he meant in a verse:

The enlightened person observes no precepts
even when tempted to do so,
And does not meditate even when alone.
After two or three cups of strong tea,
All subtle meanings exist alongside the hoe.

There is a saying: "Every road leads to Ch'ang-an." It can equally be said that "every gate opens onto Buddhism." The most important practices for entering the gate leading to Buddhahood are to keep the precepts and to sit in meditation, yet Ch'an Master Yang-shan claimed that he did neither. Did he then desert Buddhism? No, he did not. All precepts emphasize rules and regulations. This is because Ch'an stresses the freedom from all bonds rather than being restrained by forms or concepts, regardless if they are evil or pure. Hence, Master Yang-shan, after denying all such distinctions, stated: "After two or three cups of strong tea, All subtle meanings exist alongside the hoe." This implies that a real Ch'an master never strays from the middle path to either extreme, which is the true practice.

Requiting Kindness

Ch'an Master Lin-chi was about to take leave of his teacher, Ch'an Master Huang-po. The latter asked him, "Where are you going?"

"Either to Henan or to Hepei," Lin-chi answered.

Huang-po immediately slapped him. Grabbing the teacher, Lin-chi slapped him back. Although he had been struck, Huang-po laughed heartily and said to his attendant in a loud voice, "Go and get the late Master Pai-chang's Ch'an board and sutra stand[41] for me."

Lin-chi also called out, "Bring some fire, too."

Huang-po turned to Lin-chi and said, "Although I said this, the fire will not burn. Just go as you wish. Only you'll have to keep the people of the whole world quiet."

Later, when Ch'an Master Kuei-shan Ling-yu discussed this incident with Yang-shan, he asked, "Did Lin-chi insult his teacher, Huang-po, by his behavior?"

"No, not really," Yang-shan replied.

"Would you please explain?" implored Kuei-shan.

"By slapping Huang-po, Lin-chi actually acknowledged his teacher's kindness to him. Only those who acknowledge a kindness will requite it," Yang-shan explained.

"Do you know any such examples among sages or virtuous individuals in ancient times?" asked Kuei-shan.

"Yes, I do. But since they are from the distant past, I won't repeat them to you."

"But I've never heard of them. Please tell me," urged Kuei-shan.

"All right. In the *Śūrangama Sutra*, Ānanda praised the Buddha, pledging, 'I'm willing to offer my utter devotion to as many nations and people as there are dust particles.' This is called 'requiting the Buddha's kindnesses' and is an example from ancient times."

"Indeed," Kuei-shan said agreeably.

"If a disciple has only as much knowledge and experience as the master, this will decrease the master's virtues when the disciple tries to pass the teachings on. Only when one surpasses one's teacher will one be able to impart fully the teacher's wisdom."

In the Ch'an School, the teaching methods that had been passed on from Master Huang-po and Lin-chi belonged to the Lin-chi School, while those from Master Kuei-shan and Yang-shan belonged to the Kuei-yang School. These masters were all first and second generation disciples of Ch'an Master Pai-chang. Although Kuei-shan (771-853 C.E.) was five years older than Huang-po (776-856 C.E.), sixteen years older than Lin-chi, and belonged to a different school, he always held these two masters in high esteem. This is what is known as being magnanimous, virtuous, and enlightened.

Unable to Be Snatched Away

One day, Ch'an Master Lin-chi was going to work in the fields with his teacher, Master Huang-po, who was walking ahead. After a while, Huang-po turned around and saw that his student was empty-handed. "How could you forget to bring your hoe with you?" he asked.

"I don't know who took it away," explained the student.

Upon hearing this, Huang-po stopped and said, "Come over here. I have something to tell you."

When Lin-chi was in front of him, Huang-po held up his hoe and said, "'This' is something that no one in this world can take away."

Lin-chi snatched the hoe away from his teacher. While holding it tightly in his hand, Lin-chi said, "Master, you just claimed that no one could take 'this' away. Why, then, is 'this' now in my hand?"

Huang-po replied, "Although you hold 'this' in your hand, you don't necessarily have it. The fact that I'm empty-handed doesn't necessarily mean I don't possess it, either. Now, tell me, who will do the farming today?"

Lin-chi answered, "Whoever wants to plow or whoever wants to harvest, let him do it. Why should this concern us?"

Upon hearing this, Master Huang-po turned around and returned to the monastery without uttering a word.

Later, Master Kuei-shan asked Yang-shan, "The hoe was in Master Huang-po's hand; why did he let Lin-chi snatch it away?"

Yang-shan replied, "Although only a crude person takes things away by force, Lin-chi showed more wisdom than a gentleman."

Kuei-shan continued his questioning, "Why did Lin-chi say that plowing and harvesting didn't concern them?"

"What's wrong with his refusing to make distinctions?"

Kuei-shan said nothing, but turned around, and returned to the monastery.

Both Huang-po and Kuei-shan turned around, implying that they affirmed what the others had said. People in this world talk a lot when they are right. They talk even more when they are wrong. If they can turn around in front of Truth, they will be able to see an altogether different world.

Can Trees Become Buddhas?

Japanese Zen Master Chen-kuan studied the doctrine of the T'ien-t'ai School for six years, after which, he converted to the teachings of

Ch'an. Having studied the teachings for seven years, Chen-kuan went to China and traveled for twelve years through famous mountains to visit Ch'an masters and to practice meditation.

After being in the Ch'an School for more than twenty years, he finally perceived his true nature. He then packed his belongings and returned to his own country.

In the cities of Kamakura and Nara, he disseminated the Ch'an teaching far and wide. Buddhists from all over came swarming to seek instruction and to practice meditation under his guidance. They all posed questions which were difficult for him to answer. These included: (1) What is one's Buddha-nature? (2) What was the meaning of the Patriarch's coming from the West? (3) What was the meaning of Master Chao-chou's ambivalent answers when he was asked whether a dog had the Buddha-nature? Although he was asked many questions, Master Chen-kuan always kept his eyes closed and refused to answer even one of them. Some people knew that the Master did not like to discuss *kung-an*s with others. Hence, people discussed amongst themselves but did not improve their understanding of the *kung-an*s.

One day, Master Tao-wen, who was a scholar from the T'ien-t'ai School, went to visit Chen-kuan and paid his respects. Tao-wen was about fifty years old at the time and had been studying T'ien-t'ai doctrine for more than thirty years. He told Chen-kuan with great sincerity, "I've studied the *Lotus Sutra* of the T'ien-t'ai School ever since I was a child, but there's still one point I could never understand."

Chen-kuan straightforwardly retorted, "The *Lotus Sutra* is complex and profound. It is comprehensive and flawless. People who read it are supposed to have many questions. Yet you only have one! What is your question?"

Tao-wen declared, "It states in the *Lotus Sutra*: 'The sentient and the non-sentient will both attain *prajñā*.' This implies that trees, grass, and flowers can all become Buddhas. Is this possible?"

Chen-kuan replied, "Well, in the past thirty years, you've been worrying about whether trees, grass, and flowers can attain Buddhahood. What benefit will you get from knowing that? You should have concerned yourself with the question of whether you can become a Buddha."

Tao-wen was startled by this response. Finally, he said, "I've never thought of this question. May I ask, how can I become a Buddha?"

Chen-kuan answered, "You said that you only had one question, so you'll have to answer the second question yourself."

It is not important whether trees, grass, or flowers can become Buddhas. This is because the earth, mountains, rivers, trees, flowers, and all other substances originate from the same source as our own nature. If we can become Buddhas, then all phenomena will naturally become Buddhas. We should probe the root of things rather than concentrating on the ramifications, otherwise we will never enter the Path. Ch'an immediately forces us to discern our own nature rather than being distracted by other matters.

Banter between Novices

Ch'an masters from two monasteries were training their novices to arrive at incisive and timely responses that would suit the occasion and reflect the teachings of Ch'an.

Every day, both monasteries would send some of the students to buy vegetables from the market. One day, a novice from the first monastery ran into one from the rival monastery on his way to the market. The first student asked his counterpart, "Where are you going?"

"Wherever the wind carries me," he replied.

Not expecting such an answer, the first novice did not know how to continue the conversation. When he returned to his monastery, he told his master what had happened. The Master criticized him, "You fool! You could have asked, 'What if there is no wind?'"

The novice memorized the Master's instructions, and when he bumped into the other novice again the following day, he asked confidently, "Where are you going?"

"Wherever my legs carry me," the latter replied nonchalantly.

This answer was not what he had expected. Again, not knowing what to say, he returned to his master for help. The Master reprimanded him even more severely, "You're really stupid! You should have asked him, 'What if your legs don't want to walk?'"

The student memorized this response as he had done with the first response. A few days later he came across the other novice and again asked, "Where are you going?"

Pointing in the direction he was walking, the latter answered, "I'm going to the market to buy vegetables."

Since he had answered the question directly this time, the first novice still could not arrive at a response.

Although the first novice was kind and polite, he could not arrive at timely responses, whereas the second novice answered the questions humorously and with the full flavor of Ch'an. Thus, in studying Ch'an, one should not be rigid. Since Ch'an has served as a faculty of quick-thinking, people who have this wisdom will have witty remarks readily available at their fingertips.

In short, the two novices were simply going to the market to buy vegetables. However, the second novice was able to give a clever response to the other's greetings. This wonderful use of the fundamental quality of Ch'an was derived from his mastering of the mind of Ch'an. These exchanges serve as an illustration of the unique flavor of Ch'an.

Questioning the Head Monk to Death

When Ch'an Master Tung-shan met Head Monk Ch'u, the latter said, "Buddhism is so profound that it is incomprehensible."

Upon hearing this, Tung-shan said, "Let's save the question of whether Buddhism is comprehensible or not for another time. First, I would like to ask to which world do you belong?"

Head Monk Ch'u remained silent. Tung-shan did not give up and insisted, "Why don't you answer me? To which world do you belong?"

"Don't be so impatient!" retorted the Head Monk.

"How can I be patient if you won't even answer this fundamental question?"

Ch'u still would not say a word. Tung-shan continued to press for an answer, arguing, "Whether you follow the Buddha or his teaching, it is merely a matter of a name. Why don't you answer the question according to the sutras?"

Ch'u now expressed great interest and asked immediately, "What do the sutras state?"

Tung-shan replied, "According to the sutras, a Buddhist should rely on the meaning of the teaching rather than on the language. In other words, once the implication is grasped, one shouldn't try to discriminate and understand the individual words."

Ch'u objected, "You're still creating diseases (delusions) in your mind even with the help of the sutras!"

"You argued that the world of Buddhism is too abstruse to be understood," Tung-shan retorted. "What would you say about your disease of passivity and reluctance to assume responsibility?"

Ch'u again fell silent, not because he did not wish to answer, but because he could not answer. The next day, the Head Monk was found dead. Thereafter, Tung-shan was known by many practitioners in the Ch'an School as "Master Liang-chieh who questioned the Head Monk to death."

It is difficult to conclude that the monk's death has a causal relationship to Master Tung-shan's persistent questioning. Nonetheless, questions and answers in the Ch'an School are really like thunder and lightning. They take place so rapidly that one does not have time to apply any sort of reasoning. The world of Buddhism eliminates the problems of profundity and simplicity. Therefore, do we need to distinguish between these concepts?

Whipping the Cart or the Ox?

Ch'an Master Nan-yüeh Huai-jang, Abbot of the Po-jê Temple, noticed a young man meditating in the main shrine every afternoon. Since the man seemed to possess Ch'an wisdom, Huai-jang asked him kindly, "My friend, what are you doing here?"

The young man obviously did not like being disturbed and reluctantly answered, "Sitting in meditation."

"Why are you sitting in meditation?" asked Huai-jang again.

Quite perturbed, he nevertheless replied, "To become a Buddha!"

The Master continued to pursue his questioning in a kind manner, "How can you become a Buddha by sitting in meditation?"

This time, the young man ignored the question to show his disdain for the talkative old monk. Since Huai-jang could not attract the young man's attention by talking, he found a brick and began to rub it on the floor while sitting nearby. In the days that followed, whenever the young man came to meditate, Master Nan-yüeh would return to his task of rubbing the brick. Finally, the young man could no longer suppress his curiosity and inquired, "What are you doing here every day, if I may ask?"

"Polishing the brick," Huai-jang declared.

"Why?" he queried.

"To make it into a mirror," replied Huai-jang.

"How can you turn the brick into a mirror?" the young man asked.

"If the brick can't become a mirror by being polished, how can you become a Buddha by meditating?"

The young man was astounded by the response. This simple question completely rid him of his arrogance. He immediately stood up and prostrated himself respectfully before the Master, imploring, "What should I do?"

In reply, the Master asked him gently, "Let's say you're driving a cart. If it doesn't go forward, should you whip the cart or the ox?"

Upon hearing this, the young man prostrated again and then knelt down, saying, "Master, how can I be free from all bondage and attain nirvana?"

"Your study of the doctrines of the Buddha is like sowing seeds, while my expounding to you the essence of the Dharma is like sprinkling sweet dew on those seeds. When causes and conditions harmonize, you'll be awakened to the Path."

After hearing this, the young man became enlightened. Later, he became the famous Ch'an Master Ma-tsu Tao-i.

The process by which Master Ma-tsu became awakened to the Dharma proves that the aim of meditation is to enlighten the mind and behold the Buddha-nature that is within each of us. Sitting in meditation is not enough to enable one to realize that goal. This is because Ch'an does not merely imply the external posture of sitting or lying down. Ch'an cannot be confined to any fixed position. While it is true that sitting in meditation is a means of practicing Ch'an, it is not the purpose of Ch'an practice. When the wagon does not move, one should whip the ox rather than the cart, for it is the ox that is responsible. Likewise, meditation that is undertaken for the purpose of enlightenment concerns the mind rather than the body. The mind is the forerunner of everything. Cultivation of the mind is crucial to any kind of right practice.

The Flying Buddha

The Ch'i-hsia Shan Temple located in Nanking was known as a sacred place during the Six dynasties and was famous for its thousand Buddhas sculptures. Among the one thousand magnificent statues that were carved into the mountain, one was poised atop a very high peak. It stood there so solemnly that all who passed by looked up at it to pay their respects.

In 1941, a lay Buddhist visited the mountain. When he saw the statue erected on the summit, he asked his guide, Ch'an Master Cho-ch'êng, "Master, what is the name of that Buddha?"

"Flying Buddha," he said. The old monk meant that the mountain was so high that no one could have possibly climbed up and carved it, so it must have flown there from some unknown place.

"If he flew here by himself, why doesn't he fly away?"

"Because movement is not as good as stillness," the Master answered patiently.

"But why does it have to remain here?"

"Since it is here already, why shouldn't it stay and make the best of the place?" the Master questioned.

Although Master Cho-ch'êng answered these questions noncha-lantly, we can obtain great insights from them. The statement "Because movement is not as good as stillness" implies a wondrous realm of mind, while the question "Since it is here already, why shouldn't it stay and make the best of the place?" conveys a positive attitude toward life. In an ever changing world, one cannot find peace. Even when one is asleep, one's consciousness continues to function in dreams. One should realize that the state of tranquil-ity is vast and great. Only when one dwells in harmony will life be serene and meaningful. In practicing Ch'an meditation, one should remember the inspiration of the "Flying Buddha": it is better to be tranquil than to be agitated, and one should concentrate contentedly on meditation wherever one is.

Have a Pleasant Journey

One night, Ch'an Master Tung-shan Liang-chieh was expounding the Dharma in the dark. A monk named Nêng-jên asked the Master why he did not light a lamp. In response to the question, Tung-shan told an attendant to light one. Then, the Master turned to Nêng-jên and ordered, "Please come over here!"

When Nêng-jên was standing in front of him, Tung-shan said to the attendant, "Go and get three pints of lamp oil for this monk."

Did Tung-shan intend to be compassionate or sarcastic, or did he have other intentions? Nêng-jên made no reply but left the preaching hall. He pondered on the incident for the entire night and seemed to have gained a clear insight on what the Master had implied. He then took all his savings and made offerings of food for all the monastics at the temple. After staying at the monastery for three years, he told Tung-shan that he had decided to leave, and the latter did not press him to stay. The Master only said, "May you have a pleasant journey."

It happened that Master Hsüeh-fêng was standing nearby. After Nêng-jên left, he asked Tung-shan, "I wonder when this monk will return."

Tung-shan said, "Well, he knows that he can leave now, but he doesn't know when he can return. If you're worried about him, why don't you go and talk to him?"

When Hsüeh-fêng went to the monks' quarters, he found the monk dead in his seat. He hurried back to inform Tung-shan.

Upon hearing the news, Tung-shan said, "Although he only passed away just now, he died thirty years later than I did."

In this *kung-an*, Monk Nêng-jên called Master Tung-shan to account for not lighting the lamp while expounding the Dharma. It would be considered natural for people to ask for light when they are in the dark. It was also natural for Tung-shan to yield and comply with the request. What seemed extraordinary was that the Master gave the monk more than he had bargained for. Offering the monk some lamp oil may be interpreted as a sign of Tung-shan's great compassion. It may also be taken as a sarcastic comment on Nêng-jên's greediness. Whatever the Master's intentions were, the monk became enlightened. Henceforth, Nêng-

jên made food offerings to demonstrate that he had been liberated
from greed.

Afterward, Nêng-jên stayed with Tung-shan for three more
years before bidding farewell to the Master to fulfill his worldly
obligations. He then entered nirvana with the Master's best wishes.

For Ch'an Buddhists, birth and death are like returning home.
What is most intriguing is why did Tung-shan say that the monk
died thirty years later than he had while he was still alive? Well,
this is simply indication that he had comprehended that there was
no life or death thirty years ago.

Constancy Versus Inconstancy

Ch'an Master Tao-shu established a temple adjacent to a Taoist monastery. The Taoists refused to leave the neighboring temple alone. Every
day, they would either call up demons and ghosts, or summon wind and
rain, thunder and lightning, to drive out the monastics of Tao-shu's
temple. This frightened many young novices, and they quickly left.
Master Tao-shu was not the least bit disturbed. He remained in the
monastery for more than ten years. In the end, the Taoists exhausted all
their tricks and abandoned their own temple.

Later, some people asked Tao-shu, "The Taoists excel in magical
powers. How were you able to defeat them?"

"By the word wu[42]."

"How can you defeat them with this word?" they inquired.

Tao-shu explained, "They have magical powers, but to 'have'
means to be limited to existence. I don't possess any of those powers.
This wu is limitless and boundless. I understand the relationship
between 'having' and 'not having.' Therefore, I can meet all apparent
changes with steadiness. My 'constancy' is bound to beat their
'inconstancy.'"

Accepting a Gift

One day, Ch'an Master Kuei-shan Ling-yu told his disciple, Master Yang-shan, "A devotee came to me with three bolts of white silk. He asked me to strike the temple bell and pray for him. He also said that he hoped the world would achieve peace and happiness."

Yang-shan responded pointedly, "This man is so sincere about Buddhism and wants you to pray for his happiness so badly. Now that you've accepted his silk, how are you going to repay him?"

Tapping his bed with his staff three times, Ling-yu replied, "I will repay him with this."

Yang-shan was not satisfied with the answer, "What's the use of 'this'?"

Ling-yu touched the bed three more times, inquiring, "Are you saying that 'this' is not enough?"

Yang-shan explained, "It's not that I object to 'this,' but 'this' belongs to everybody. I don't think that our master should repay him with something owned by all of us."

Ling-yu retorted, "If you know 'this' belongs to all of us, why do you still ask me to give him something else? Tell me, besides 'this,' how else can I thank him?"

Yang-shan said disapprovingly, "If the devotee has already gotten 'this,' why should he still trouble others to give it to him?"

"Although he has 'this,' without the help of others, how can he recognize that he has it? Don't you remember when Bodhidharma came to our country, he also gave our countrymen 'this'? Thus, all Ch'an Buddhists are recipients of his gift!"

What is 'this'? It is one's own Buddha-nature. If one has it, why does one still need to be granted 'this'? The answer to such a sensible question is that "being granted" refers to the assistance of teachers. Without their help, it would be difficult for one to behold this nature. The Buddhist sutras serve the same function. It is true that the Ch'an School does "not set up scriptures" but focuses on the true mind and on beholding the Buddha-nature that is within oneself. Without the sutras, how can one learn to behold one's own Buddha-nature and become enlightened? The *sutras* are the means, not the end. It is just like crossing a river by means of a boat. How

can one abandon the boat before one gets across the river? Once a person reaches the other shore, the person should not hesitate to discard the boat and continue the journey. Whereas Kuei-shan discussed "this" from the perspective of education, Yang-shan discussed it in terms of his personal experience. Nevertheless, they both shared the same fundamental insight.

The Peerless Dharma Treasure

Bodhidharma's given name was Bodhitara. He was the third son of a Brahman king in southern India. His teacher, Prajñātāra, regarded him highly, encouraged him to take on a monastic life, and gave him a new name, Bodhidharma.

While still at home, Bodhidharma already displayed extraordinary wisdom and exceptional virtue. Once, Venerable Prajñātāra pointed to a pile of pearls and jewels and asked the three brothers of the family, "Is there anything in this world more precious than jewels?"

"No, there isn't," said the eldest brother. "These pearls and jewels are the most precious objects for royal families like ours. Nothing can be found on Earth that will be more valuable than they are."

The second brother echoed this opinion. "He's right. I've never seen anything in my life that is more valuable."

However, the third brother, Bodhitara, disagreed, "I don't think my two elder brothers are correct. These jewels actually don't have much value."

The other two exclaimed together, "Why not? Show us a more valuable treasure!"

Bodhitara explained, "I say this because the pearls and jewels can't see their own value. They have to rely on human wisdom to perceive it, since they, themselves, are merely inanimate objects. The Dharma preached by the Buddha is the Truth, which is the wisdom radiating from human enlightenment. It is not only self-illuminating, but it also can distinguish between various kinds of jewels. Moreover, it can differentiate between good and evil that exist in and beyond this world. Therefore, among all the treasures, the most precious is the peerless treasure of the Dharma."

Bodhidharma's wisdom transcended all conventions. With such a superior perspective, he was able to inherit the robe and alms-bowl of Prajñātāra, and Bodhidharma became the twenty-eighth Buddhist patriarch in India. During the reign of Emperor Wu (464-549 C.E.) of the Liang dynasty, he traveled to China and stayed in a monastery in Sung Shan. It was said that he sat facing a wall at the monastery for nine years. He was recognized as the founder of Ch'an Buddhism in China.

What are the real treasures in life? In this world, there are material treasures such as gold, silver, pearls, and so forth, while beyond this world, there are three—the Three Precious Ones. Each of these has its own characteristic: Buddha is wisdom; Dharma is righteousness; and *Sangha* is purity. These treasures make up the Buddha-nature that is inherent in every individual. Gold, silver, and jewels can lose their sheen with age, but this original nature neither gains nor loses. Bodhitara realized this when he was still a child. Hence, he was a fitting successor to his teacher and went east to preach the Dharma. This proves that gold, silver, and other worldly treasures are no comparison to the treasure of the Dharma.

How Much Does It Weigh?

Su Tung-p'o, a scholar of the Imperial Academy, once debated with Ch'an Master Chao-chüeh about the Path to enlightenment. During the debate, they touched upon the question of whether both sentient and non-sentient beings could attain perfect wisdom. Inspired by the discussion, Su wrote three poems to express what he had learned. Their titles were "Before Practicing Ch'an," "While Practicing Ch'an," and "After Becoming Enlightened through the Practice of Ch'an."

The first poem read as follows:

> Viewed horizontally, it is a mountain range;
> while viewed vertically, it becomes a peak.
> Far and near, high and low—each is unique.
> The real face of Lu Shan is not to be seen,
> Because one is standing on the mountain.

The second poem expressed a different state of mind, while Su engaged in Ch'an practice:

> The misty rain of Lu Shan and the tides of
>   Chekiang,
> Not seeing them in person is forever re-
>   grettable.
> After arriving, nothing unusual is to be
>   seen—
> The misty rain of Lu Shan and the tides of
>   Chekiang.

The final poem described Su's feelings after he had attained realization through Ch'an practice:

> The sounds of rippling creeks are long,
>   wide tongues;
> The mountains are the pure bodies of the
>   Buddhas.
> Late at night, when contemplating the 84,000
>   verses,
> How is one to explain what one has realized?

After this experience, Su Tung-p'o thought even more highly of his own understanding of the Dharma. When he was told that Ch'an Master Ch'êng-hao from Yu-ch'üan Temple in Chingnan was so incisive that his timely questions defied response, Su Tung-p'o refused to believe it. He went to visit the Master in civilian clothing to test the latter's knowledge of Ch'an. As soon as he met the Master, he asked, "I was told that you're very good at Ch'an meditation. May I ask, what is meditation?"

The Master did not answer Su Tung-p'o's question, but instead asked, "Sir, may I have your name, please?"

Su Tung-p'o replied, "My name is Scale, which weighs all the abbots who are on Earth."

Upon hearing this, the Master gave a loud shout and asked, "May I ask how much that shout weighs?"

Su Tung-p'o had nothing to say in reply, but simply stood up, prostrated, and left.

In meditation, Su Tung-p'o experienced the three stages described by Ch'an Master Ch'ing-yüan Hsing-ssǔ: "When one sees a mountain or a river before practicing Ch'an, it is simply a mountain or a river. When one sees a mountain or a river during Ch'an practice, it neither looks like a mountain nor a river. When one sees a mountain or a river after practicing Ch'an, it is again a mountain or a river."

After progressing through these three stages, one acquires a comprehension of the Dharma, however, one still will not be enlightened, for one has yet to attain a realization of what one has understood through personal experience. In other words, a Ch'an practitioner's self-cultivation starts by comprehending the Truth and is perfected by practicing the Truth. A person who lacks either self-cultivation or realization will surely become dumbfounded and speechless by a shout from Ch'an masters such as Ch'êng-hao.

Kicked by a Donkey

Ch'an Master Chao-chou had always led a carefree life. Following his inclinations, he was able to adapt himself to different circumstances. Lacking a permanent home, he was still able to feel at home wherever he went. He wandered far and wide, even when he was over eighty years old. Later, someone wrote a poem about Master Chao-chou:

> At eighty, Chao-chou still wandered,
> Because something in his mind was not
>   settled.
> But upon returning, nothing had been
>   gained,
> By then he realized that he had wasted money
>   on his straw sandals.

One day, he went to Ch'an Master Yün-chü's temple. Yün-chü asked him, "At such an old age, you're still a roving monk? Why don't you find a place to make it your permanent home?"

"Where could my permanent home be?" Chao-chou asked, as if he had not understood the question.

"There is a deserted temple near the mountain. You can renovate it and live there."

But Chao-chou was not at all interested. In reply, he asked, "Old monk, why don't you go and live there?"

Another time, Chao-chou arrived at Master Chu-yü's temple. Chu-yü asked him the same question, "You're so old, and you're still wandering around. Why don't you find a place to settle down and practice peacefully?"

"Where do you think I can find such a place?" asked Chao-chou excitedly.

Chu-yü objected to this question, "You shouldn't ask others for an answer. At such an advanced age, you don't even know where you can live. How can you talk like this?"

Upon hearing this, Chao-chou could not help but feel a tremendous respect for Master Chu-yü. He said, "For thirty years, I've been on horseback galloping across mountains and rivers and have lived in accordance with circumstances. Who would have thought that I would be kicked by a donkey today?"

Master Chao-chou first began wandering because a monk once asked him, "When the fire in the age of degeneration burns, will it destroy our physical bodies, which are made of the four elements and the five aggregates?" Chao-chou answered, "Yes." The monk continued, "If so, should we allow the body to follow its own inclinations?" "Yes," Chao-chou affirmed. The monk had doubts about Chao-chou's reply. Even Chao-chou, himself, began to wonder if his reply was correct, so he started traveling. He visited Ch'an masters everywhere in order to resolve his doubts. Actually, Chao-chou had already found his permanent home through his travels. Thus, in the above vignette, the "donkey's kick" was merely a reminder that he should practice diligently.

Being Able to Forget Is Difficult

Master Chao-chou asked Kuei-shan Ling-yu, "What's the intention of the Ch'an patriarchs of all generations?"

Kuei-shan ordered his attendant, "Go and get a chair!"

Chao-chou continued, "Since I became the abbot of the monastery, I've never met a real Ch'an practitioner."

A novice monk happened to be present. He immediately asked Chao-chou, "What will you do if you bump into one?"

"I won't shoot my arrow at a rat that is in a ditch."

"Who is the master of all Buddhas?" the novice continued.

"Amitābha," Chao-chou replied.

"Who's he?" the novice asked again.

"He's my disciple!" declared Chao-chou.

Later, the novice told another Ch'an master, Ch'ang-ch'ing, about this conversation. He asked, "Master Chao-chou said Amitābha was his disciple. Did he mean to lead me further into the conversation, or had he given up on me?"

"Well, if you probe into both ends of his words, you'll miss the real meaning," Ch'ang-ch'ing answered.

"What was the real meaning?" inquired the novice.

The Master snapped his fingers. The novice had no idea what this meant and continued to study under Chao-chou.

Once, the monarch of the State of Chao invited Chao-chou to expound the Dharma. As soon as he got on the platform, he began to chant the sutras. The novice was surprised and whispered, "Master, you're supposed to talk about the Dharma. Why are you chanting?"

"Can't disciples of the Buddha chant sutras?" retorted Chao-chou.

Later, when everyone in the monastery was chanting, Chao-chou sat straight up with his mouth closed. When the novice saw this, he asked, "Master, why aren't you chanting?"

Chao-chou answered, "Thank you for mentioning the term 'chanting.' I almost forgot about it."

In the history of the Ch'an School, Chao-chou was a very humorous figure. He would not shoot an arrow to kill a rat and claimed to be the teacher of Amitābha. When he was invited to give a lecture on the Dharma, he chanted. While others were chanting, he meditated.

He did not deliberately speak and act contrary to others. His actions implied that Ch'an practitioners ought to be detached and should be able to "forget." One ought to forget self, others, feelings, surroundings, right, wrong, having, and not having.

A Lion Roaring on a Rock

The second morning after Ch'an Master Shih-t'ou Hsi-ch'ien arrived at Nan-tai Temple, he said to Master Huai-jang, "When I came yesterday, I saw an absurd young Ch'an monk sitting motionless on a rock."

"Are you sure that you saw him?" queried Huai-jang.

"Yes, I am," Master Shih-t'ou declared.

Afterward, Huai-jang said to his attendant, "Go and find out who that young man was. If he's the same monk who arrived yesterday, ask him what trick he's playing. If he admits to being the young monk on the rock, ask him: 'Can something that is growing on a rock survive after being transplanted?'"

The attendant went to Shih-t'ou and repeated what Huai-jang had said. Shih-t'ou replied, "In the world of all Buddhas, nothing can be moved, and neither death nor life exists."

The attendant reported Shih-t'ou's words, and Huai-jang mumbled to himself, "I'm sure his descendants will make the people on Earth mute out of awe."

He then sent his attendant back to Shih-t'ou with more questions. "How can we be really free from all bonds?"

Shih-t'ou asked in reply, "But who has bound you?"

"How can we reach the Pure Land?" inquired the attendant.

"But who has contaminated you?" Shih-t'ou responded.

"What exactly is nirvana?" questioned the attendant.

"Who has given you life and death?" Shih-t'ou continued.

When Master Huai-jang heard the detailed report of Shih-t'ou's answers, he joined his palms together without uttering a word.

Ch'ing-yüan Hsing-ssǔ and Nan-yüeh Huai-jang, who were prominent Ch'an masters, were favorite disciples of Master Hui-nêng. Both held: "You can hear a lion roaring on a rock[43]."

Master Hsi-ch'ien's questions reflected the Sixth Patriarch's conception—since there was nothing to begin with, dust could not alight. The so-called state of "being bound" had the implication of self-bondage. Similarly, one would be responsible for one's delusion. Living or dying would also be the result of one's choosing to sink into the ocean of misery of life and death. Similarly, a rock does not initiate movement, nor does it experience life or death. Nevertheless, we have insisted on worrying about these problems, which have arisen simply from our own imagination. Hence, Master Hui-jang told us to listen to the lion's roar, referring to the powerful preaching of enlightened Ch'an masters.

The Unchangeable Former Debts

When Emperor Wu-tsung (814-846 C.E.) of the T'ang dynasty was persecuting Buddhists, Ch'an Master Yen-t'ou had some secular clothing made for possible emergencies. Soon afterward, an imperial edict was issued to all monasteries, ordering monks and nuns to return to secular life. Worse still, well-known senior monastics were to be arrested and sentenced. To protect himself from the tyranny, Yen-t'ou put on his layman's clothes and cap and hid in a lay Buddhist shrine. It just so happened that the abbess was having a meal in the dining room when Yen-t'ou arrived. Yen-t'ou swaggered into the kitchen, took a bowl and a pair of chopsticks, and began eating. A young novice saw him and immediately told the abbess about it. She came in with a big pole and assumed a fighting stance, only to realize whom she had confronted. Surprised, she inquired, "Oh, it is Abbot Yen-t'ou. Why did you change into lay clothes?"

Master Yen-t'ou replied calmly, "Although outer form can be changed, the nature underlying the appearance remains the same."

Later Ch'an Master Ta-yen visited Yen-t'ou. When he arrived, Yen-t'ou was weeding in front of the door. Ta-yen strutted over, wearing a straw hat on his head. Standing directly in front of Yen-t'ou, Ta-yen touched his hat with his hand and asked, "Do you still remember me?"

Yen-t'ou threw some grass at Ta-yen's face, commenting, "The world is changing constantly. How can I remember you?"

Ta-yen was not about to give in so easily and argued, "The world is changeable, while the Dharma-nature is eternal. How can you forget your debts?"

Upon hearing this, Yen-t'ou slapped Ta-yen three times. Ta-yen teetered precariously, regained his balance, and walked off. He was ready to enter the preaching hall when Yen-t'ou again said, "Since we've already exchanged greetings, there's no need for you to go inside."

Ta-yen immediately turned around and left. The next morning, he returned to the preaching hall again after breakfast. As soon as he walked through the door, Yen-t'ou jumped off his seat and caught hold of him, shouting, "Out with it! Out with it! Where are the unchangeable former debts?"

Ta-yen also grabbed him, "In the lay Buddhist's house."

They both laughed heartily.

The forms of all phenomena arise, change, and become extinct, but they do not apply to the Dharma-nature. In other words, the world goes through the stages of origination, duration, degeneration, and dissolution. Human beings go through a similar cycle—birth, aging, illness, and death. The mind, in turn, evolves through such a cycle. Only our true nature is everlasting and fresh. When there was no freedom of religious belief under the tyrannical government, Master Yen-t'ou exchanged his robes for a layman's clothes, yet his self-existing, fundamental, pure mind remained immutable. In other words, gold can be carved into rings, earrings, and bracelets, but its nature remains the same. Although human beings can transmigrate between the five realms of hells, hungry ghosts, animals, humans, and deities—their true nature will nonetheless remain the same.

A Tiger Grows Horns

One day, Ch'an Master Huang-po Hsi-ch'ien went into the kitchen and asked the cook, "What are you doing?"

"I'm cooking rice for everyone at the temple."

"How much do we eat everyday?" asked Huang-po.

"About 275 pounds each day."

"Isn't that too much?" Huang-po asked again.

"Oh, no. I'm afraid that it is not enough," stated the cook.

After hearing this, Huang-po raised his hand and slapped the cook on the face. The cook later told Master Lin-chi about the incident.

Lin-chi did not think that the cook had said anything to deserve the slapping. To comfort the cook, he said, "I'm going to ask the old monk why he did this to you."

When he got there, Huang-po took the initiative in relating what had happened between the cook and himself. After he finished, Lin-chi said, "The cook wants me to ask you why you slapped him because he can't figure it out."

"Why do you think I slapped him?" Huang-po asked in reply.

Lin-chi expressed his disagreement with Huang-po, "I don't see anything wrong with worrying about whether there was enough rice."

"But why didn't he say 'We'll have another meal tomorrow' instead?" argued Huang-po.

Lin-chi raised his fist and cried out, "Forget about tomorrow. We want to eat right now!" As he said this, he struck Huang-po.

The latter pushed him away with reproach, "You crazy monk! You're trying to pull the tiger's beard again!"

Upon hearing this, Lin-chi left the preaching hall, roaring. Huang-po was pleased by Lin-chi's behavior and said to himself, "This little tiger has grown horns on his head."

Later, when Ch'an Master Kuei-shan Ling-yu was discussing this incident with Yang-shan Hui-chi, he asked, "How do you explain what happened between those two masters?"

"What's your opinion, Master?" asked Yang-shan.

"Only after the parents have given birth to a child will the depth of parental affection be fully understood," Kuei-shan answered.

"I don't think so," Yang-shan said.

"What's your opinion then?" Kuei-shan queried.

"I think what happened between the two was just like someone allowing a thief into one's own house to steal one's own belongings."

Upon hearing this, Master Kuei-shan laughed heartily.

It is considered a preposterous act for a student to beat a teacher. Yet, Huang-po was not offended by what Lin-chi had done. On the

contrary, he complimented him. According to a Chinese saying: "Beating is none other than parental affection, while scolding is none other than an expression of intimacy and love." This is even more meaningful in the context of the Ch'an School.

I Don't Have a Mouth

There was a novice named Tao-nien who had been a monk for several decades, and he visited Ch'an masters everywhere. Still, he could not become enlightened. One day, he went to Master Shi-lou for help, "Master, I can't behold my original nature. I implore you to instruct me."

"But I don't have a mouth," replied Shi-lou.

"I'm ready to listen to you with utmost sincerity and respectful attention," Tao-nien implored again.

"What do you want to hear?" asked the Master.

"I know that I have created a lot of negative karma due to previous wrong doings," answered Tao-nien.

"I also have a lot of wrong doings," said the Master.

"What are they, Master?" asked Tao-nien.

"My wrong doings are the same as yours," answered Shi-lou.

"Master, can we repent for our wrong doings?" inquired Tao-nien.

Shi-lou answered, "All wrong doings don't have an ultimate reality. They come from the [illusory] mind. If the [illusory] mind is extinguished, all wrong doings will naturally be extinguished."

Upon hearing this, Tao-nien prostrated. Master Shi-lou struck him and then asked, "Where did you travel before you came here?"

"I wandered all over the country throughout the Five dynasties," answered Tao-nien.

"Do the rulers of these dynasties respect the Dharma?"

The novice answered, "Fortunately, you're asking me this question. If you asked others, you would have been in trouble."

"Why?" inquired the Master.

"Because these rulers don't like people to question their beliefs." explained Tao-nien.

"If they don't even allow people to ask questions, how can they be expected to respect the Dharma?" asked the Master.

"Could you please tell me how to respect the Dharma, Master?" Tao-nien asked.

Shi-lou did not answer his question. Instead, he asked, "How long ago did you receive the precepts and become a monk?"

"More than ten years ago," said Tao-nien.

"After such a long time, you still don't know how to respect the Dharma. How can I clearly explain it to you? Also, how can you hear what I would say, even if I said it?"

Upon hearing this, the novice finally attained realization.

Although Tao-nien had sought to attain enlightenment for decades, he had not been successful. When the right causal condition presented itself, he attained it effortlessly. When Master Shi-lou told him that he did not have a mouth, he meant that Ch'an requires meditation without the aid of words. Tao-nien said that he would listen to the Master with respectful attention. If he could not listen with his mind, how could he hear? Master Shi-lou pointed this out bluntly and thus dispersed the mist that had clouded Tao-nien's mind.

Love and Hate

Wen-tao, a roving monk, had long admired Ch'an Master Hui-hsün. Therefore, he went to the trouble of traveling a long distance over mountains and rivers to meet the Master. When he arrived at the cave where Hui-hsün lived, he said, "Master, I've always venerated you for your virtue. Therefore, I made this special trip so that I may be close to you and attend to your needs. Master, please be compassionate and reveal the Truth to me."

Since it was already late, Hui-hsün said to him, "The day is waning. Please stay here for the night."

When Wen-tao woke up the next morning, Master Hui-hsün had already prepared breakfast. They were about to eat when they realized that there were no extra bowls and chopsticks for Wen-tao. Without thinking, Hui-hsün picked up a human skull from outside the cave, filled it with porridge and passed it to Wen-tao. When the latter hesitated to take it, the Master said, "Your mind doesn't want to seek enlightenment. I don't think that you have come here for the Dharma. If you react to situations with erroneous feelings of love and hate or cleanliness and filthiness, how can you attain enlightenment?"

Good or evil, gain or loss, right or wrong, clean or dirty; this is the world as perceived by those who are attached to discriminating knowledge. Wen-tao approached situations with thoughts of love and hate, and thus, he refused to accept the porridge that Master Hui-hsün had handed him. Naturally, he was berated for lacking the true intention of becoming enlightened.

The Lion's Roar

Ch'an Master Ching-shan had five hundred novices, but very few of them studied earnestly. To correct this situation, Ch'an Master Huang-po decided to send Master Lin-chi to Ching-shan. Before Lin-chi left, Huang-po asked him, "What will you do when you get there?"

"I'll show them what I'll do when I get there," answered Lin-chi.

When he arrived at Ching-shan's monastery, Lin-chi went directly into the preaching hall to meet the Master. Ching-shan barely had a chance to raise his head when he heard Lin-chi let out a mighty roar. As Master Ching-shan was about to greet Lin-chi, the latter turned around abruptly and left.

One of the novices asked Ching-shan, "What did that master tell you just now? Why did he dare to shout at you?"

"He's a disciple of Master Huang-po. If you want to know why he shouted, why don't you go and ask him?"

"Well, we don't know how to ask him," replied the novice.

"Can you let out a roar, too?" asked the Master in reply.

"Yes. That's easy," the novices answered all at once.

Upon hearing this, Ching-shan immediately let out a cry and asked, "What does this cry mean?"

The students looked at each other without knowing what to say. Ching-shan continued, "That roar spreads up into heaven and down to hell. It echoes in the ten directions and shrouds the past, the present, and the future. Most of you are undisciplined and seek ease and comfort. How can you understand the lion's roar?"

After this incident, most of the five hundred novices departed from Ching-shan and began wandering to seek Ch'an instruction elsewhere.

In the Ch'an School, Master Ching-shan was an accomplished monk of deep and profound insight. However, he had not developed a teaching method to convey his message expediently. Master Lin-chi's deafening roar helped Ching-shan gain a clearer perspective. When instructing disciples, it might not be difficult for Ch'an masters to teach the fundamentals. At the same time, different students have different needs, and therefore, it might not be appropriate to teach all students by employing one and only one method. Consequently, Ching-shan also let out a roar to disperse his disciples, who could thereafter be free to wander and find places that would be appropriate for them to study. From ancient times, although virtuous Ch'an practitioners may differ in their individual personality, they had one thing in common—they never cheated or misled students.

Coming from the West

When Ch'an Master Lung-ya Chü-tun was studying under the guidance of Master Lin-chi, he asked, "What was the meaning of the Patriarch's coming from the West?"

Lin-chi did not answer his question but ordered, "Pass me the board." Lung-ya did as he was told. As soon as he got hold of the board, Lin-chi began hitting Lung-ya with it.

Lung-ya pleaded, "Oh, Master! I don't mind your beatings, but you have to tell me the meaning of the Patriarch's coming from the West."

"Hasn't the board answered your question already?" asked Lin-chi in reply.

Later, when he went to Master Ts'ui-wei Wu-hsüeh's monastery, Lung-ya asked again, "What was the meaning of the Patriarch's coming from the West?"

Master Ts'ui-wei said in reply, "Pass me the rush cushion." As soon as the Master had it in hand, he struck Lung-ya with it.

"Beat me later, Master," Lung-ya implore. "Answer my question first, please."

"Hasn't the rush cushion answered it already?" Ts'ui-wei asked.

After meditating for many years, Lung-ya finally understood the meaning of the Patriarch's coming from the West, as revealed by the board and the rush cushion.

One day, a novice asked Lung-ya, "Master, when you were roving, you visited two virtuous monks, Lin-chi and Tsui-wei. How did you like them?"

"Well, my first impressions of them are good except for the fact that they didn't tell me the underlying meaning behind the Patriarch's coming from the West," replied the Master.

"Why didn't they tell you?" inquired the novice.

"Because the board and the rush cushion had already done that," answered Lung-ya jokingly.

The Ch'an School often employs inanimate objects commonly used by Ch'an practitioners to symbolize the Buddha-truth. For example, in the practice of passing on robes and alms bowls, the two objects represent the teaching of Ch'an. Similarly, to beat someone with the board is the way to bestow Ch'an on them. From that perspective, the board represents the underlying meaning behind the Patriarch's coming from the West. A rush cushion is used in worship, and thus, symbolizes the integration of a layperson's mind with that of the Buddha. In that sense, the rush cushion can also tell about the meaning of the Patriarch's coming from the West. However, only those who have undergone prolonged and earnest meditation will understand the meaning of the Patriarch's coming from the West through the board and the rush cushion.

To Be Buried Alive Together

One day, Ch'an Master Lin-chi I-hsüan joined the other monks by going to work in the fields. On his way there he saw Master Huang-po approaching from a distance. He immediately stopped and stood there while leaning on his hoe. As Huang-po came closer, he saw Lin-chi. Huang-po asked, "Are you tired?"

Lin-chi answered, "I haven't even started working yet. How could you ask me such a question?"

Without uttering another word, Huang-po raised his monk's staff to beat Lin-chi. However, Lin-chi nimbly caught hold of it and forced Huang-po to the ground. When Lin-chi realized what he had done, he immediately bent over and said to Huang-po, "I'm sorry that I pushed you. Let me help you up."

Huang-po refused his offer, protesting, "It's not necessary. I didn't move at all. Why should I need you to help me up?"

Lin-chi withdrew his hands and walked away.

Then he heard Huang-po, shouting, "Head monk! Head monk![44] Come and help me."

While helping Huang-po, the head monk shouted angrily, "Master! How can you forgive this discourteous Lin-chi?"

As soon as Huang-po got up, he responded by hitting the head monk. By this time Lin-chi was hoeing in the field nearby, and he remarked, "Cremation is common in many places. Here we are buried alive together." The connotation of this remark was that in Ch'an meditation, one should eliminate the habit of discriminating between phenomena of movement and stillness, coming and going, and honor and disgrace.

Later, when Ch'an Master Kuei-shan heard of this incident, he asked Master Yang-shan, "What was Huang-po's intention when he beat the head monk?"

"To let the real thief escape while beating the one who tried to catch the thief," answered Yang-shan. What he meant was that those who were unenlightened were always beaten, while those who were free of care remained untouched.

We should not judge the beating and scolding that occur in the Ch'an School by secular standards. Those were methods that Ch'an

masters employed to teach their disciples. Thus, when Master
Huang-po had beaten Lin-chi with a staff, he meant to transmit the
essence of Ch'an to him. Lin-chi pushed him away to demonstrate
that he had already acquired it and that there was no need to
transmit it any more. When Huang-po refused Lin-chi's offer to
help him up, he meant that he had been in the absolute state of
perfect stillness. Thus, he needed no help. As for the head monk, he
was beaten because he spoke out of turn—he did not understand
the Master's Ch'an mind.

A Poem

Ch'an Master Shuang-hsi Pu-na and Master Ch'i-sung were close
friends. Their friendship reached the stage at which their minds merged
through Ch'an. One day, in jest, Ch'i-sung wrote a poem to mourn for
Pu-na, who was still alive and healthy.

> I am the one who should inherit your teaching,
> For conditions of life are governed by actions.
> You have always trodden on the Path;
> Knowing the illness, treatment is not
>   necessary.
> No writing can describe your appearance;
> Your lofty feelings are beyond common
>   people's imagination.
> Wherever the cloud of compassion pervades,
> The lonely moon sits at ease.

Master Pu-na was pleased and wrote a poem in response:

> Who else shares my understanding of the
>   Path but you?
> You are the only bosom friend in my life.
> Although I did not intend for us to part,
> I'll take my leave rather than miss the chance
>   to make your poem come true.

After he finished, Master Pu-na set aside the writing brush and passed away while sitting on his chair.

Master Pu-na passed away intentionally, because he was concerned about his friend's reputation in relation to his poem. The friendship between Ch'an masters was so important that they were willing to sacrifice their lives for it. Such actions cannot be performed by everyone, hence they are worthy of esteem.

In ancient times, people sometimes expressed their gratitude to their friends by their own death, to fulfill an obligation. Master Pu-na died to uphold his friend's name, based on a joke. In his poem, Master Ch'i-sung indicated his intention to take over what Master Pu-na had been doing—disseminating the Buddha-truth. Regardless of whether Ch'i-sung was joking, Pu-na approved and died without hesitation. Those who do not understand friendship between Ch'an masters may think that Pu-na was forced to die by Ch'i-sung. In fact, Ch'an masters have a thorough comprehension of life and death. As soon as they have found someone to whom they can transmit the Buddha-truth, they will immediately enter eternal rest. Could there be anything better than being so free and relaxed?

A Practitioner of No-mind

A devotee asked Ch'an Master Fo-kuang, "It states in the sutras that worshipping thousands of Buddhas is not as good as supporting one practitioner of no-mind. I wonder what's wrong with those Buddhas and what special virtues such a practitioner has."

Fo-kuang answered with a verse:

> One fleecy white cloud hovering over the
>   valley;
> Who knows how many birds will get lost on
>   their journey home?

This verse simply implies that when one makes offerings to all

Buddhas, one might mistake worshipping them for one's goal. Therefore, the individual would be likely to lose sight of oneself. If one
supports a practitioner of no-mind, one's own mind will be free from
all discriminations, affection, and feelings. Therefore, although there
was nothing wrong with the thousands of Buddhas, supporting the
practitioner of no-mind would give a person the opportunity to behold
the Buddha-nature.

With his first question answered, the devotee went on to ask, "If
Buddhist monasteries should be peaceful and quiet, why do monastics
beat the wooden fish and the drum?"

Again, Master Fo-kuang replied with a verse:

> The beating of the wooden fish and drum
>   resounds beyond the heavens.
> Thus, it saves one the trouble of meeting the
>   doorkeeper of Lung-man[45].

The beating of the wooden fish in a quiet monastery has a very
profound implication. When a fish swims in the water, it never closes
its eyes. Thus, the wooden fish represents zealous practice. Beating the
drum, on the other hand, symbolizes putting an end to karma and
bringing forth happiness. If "the beating of the wooden fish and drum/
resounds beyond the heavens," there is no need to endure the misery of
ceaseless cycles of existence.

The devotee then asked his third question, "If one can study Buddhism as a lay person, why does one need to take on the monastic life
and wear the monastics' robe?"

Master Fo-kuang's third verse was as follows:

> Although a peacock is gloriously adorned
>   with beautiful colors,
> It cannot fly as far as a swan.

In other words, it would be acceptable to pursue self-cultivation as a lay
person, but one can concentrate better if one takes on the monastic life
and becomes a monk or nun.

Master Fo-kuang thus clarified all the doubts of the lay follower.

**Before one finds answers to certain questions, one often feels that
there are thousands of unsolved questions in one's mind. With some**

explanation, the heavy mist will be dispelled and the blue sky will be revealed. In the Ch'an School, sometimes no explanation is provided. Other times, explanations involve irrelevant ideas. If one can understand the underlying implications, one will be able to recognize Ch'an in every action.

True Friendship

Ch'an Master Yao-shan Wei-cheng from Ching-t'u Temple in Hangchou strictly observed monastic discipline. He had supervised County Magistrate Li Ao's conversion to Buddhism, and he had explained the implication of an unusual clam shell containing the image of Kuan-yin to Emperor Wen-tsung of the T'ang dynasty. But he was never interested in seeking fame, nor was he interested in socializing. Although many courtiers vied with each other to make offerings to him, he always found some excuse to refuse.

The Master and Assistant Minister Chiang were on intimate terms. One day, Chiang told Master Wei-cheng, "Tomorrow, some close friends of mine will be having a gathering at my house. They're all famous scholars of our times. I earnestly request you to join us and give us a lecture on Buddhism. It would be a great honor for all of us."

Master Wei-cheng wanted to refuse, but Chiang insisted. In the end, he reluctantly agreed to attend. But when Chiang sent people to meet with the Master the next morning, they could not find him in the monastery. What they found was a note which read:

> Yesterday, I promised to attend today's party,
> But I reconsidered afterwards;
> Being a monk, I am more comfortable stay-
>   ing in a cave;
> A banquet with the state officials does not
>   suit me.

When the attendants gave Chiang the poem, he did not blame the Master for breaking his promise or being disrespectful. Instead, he respected him even more and considered him as a true friend.

Monastics vary in their dispositions. Some are determined to propagate the Buddhist teaching in all walks of life and to save all beings, while others like to live in mountains and forests. The difference results from the different vows of compassion that each individual has taken.

Śākyamuni Buddha often was found in the company of princes, dukes, and ministers. He also allowed his disciple, Mahākāśyapa, to meditate on mountains or by rivers.

Masters in the Ch'an School have different styles. Some prefer to live in seclusion, while others choose an active role in teaching Buddhism. They share the belief that Buddhism is beneficial to all humankind.

Present Your Mind to Me

When Master Pao-t'ung first visited Ch'an Master Shih-t'ou, the latter asked, "What is your mind?"

Pao-t'ung answered, "The one that can be expressed by words."

Shih-t'ou objected to this statement, "But such a mind is a false one. Your real mind can't be shown through words."

Ashamed, Pao-t'ung meditated for days and nights in search of his real mind. After ten days, he went to consult Shih-t'ou again, "Last time, I was wrong. Now I know what my real mind is."

"What is it?" asked Shih-t'ou.

"Lifting the eyebrows and blinking the eyes!" Pao-t'ung exclaimed.

Shih-t'ou persisted, "Put this aside and present your mind to me." This meant that the mind was not the movement of lifting the eyebrows and blinking the eyes.

"Then I've no mind to present," answered Pao-t'ung.

Master Shih-t'ou said in a loud voice, "Beings all have minds. Claiming that they don't is just a little short of slander. It's true that seeing and hearing, feeling and perceiving, are all parts of the false mind. Without a mind, how can one enter the Path leading to the Truth?"

Pao-t'ung finally attained realization.

The "mind" should be free from all forms such as words or movements. It should be especially free from all false thoughts and reasoning. It would be inappropriate to describe such a mind as either empty or not empty. This is what was implied in the Sixth Patriarch's statement: "Thinking of neither good nor evil—what is your true face?"

Why do Ch'an masters often say that mindlessness is the Ch'an mind? The answer is simply because our minds are delusory, which wander sometimes to heaven and sometimes to hell. Sometimes our minds take several round trips between heaven and hell in the course of one day. Thus, if Ch'an practitioners can remain in a mindless state, their real minds, free of all illusions, will emerge. The *Diamond Sutra* states: "One should produce a mind that abides nowhere."

Kuan-yin in a Clam Shell

Emperor Wen-tsung of the T'ang dynasty liked to eat clams. Fishermen along the coasts often sent gifts of clams to the Imperial Palace as tribute to the Emperor. Once, the cook found a figure that resembled Kuan-yin in a clam shell. Since it was such a vivid and solemn image, the emperor had it put in a treasure box inset with beautiful silk. It then was placed in Hsing-shan Temple for people to pay homage. Finding the figure of Kuan-yin in a clam was most unusual. Thus, the Emperor asked his officials, "Gentlemen, do any of you know what propitious omen the figure in the shell represents?"

One answered, "This is something beyond the understanding of worldly scholars. There is a Ch'an master, Yao-shan Wei-cheng, in T'ai-i Shan, who is well-versed in Buddhism. He also is possessed of broad learning and a phenomenal memory. If Your Majesty wants to find out the significance of the figure, you may have to send for him."

When the Master was called in, he told the Emperor, "Everything appears in response to something else. This figure is intended to strengthen your belief. The *Lotus Sutra* states that for those who should be saved by a bodhisattva, one would emerge to expound the Dharma to them in person. This is happening to you now, Your Majesty."

"Although the Bodhisattva has appeared, I haven't heard the explanation of the Dharma," said Wen-tsung.

"Do you think this sacred figure in the clam will inspire your belief, Your Majesty?" asked Master Wei-cheng.

"I have seen this unusual thing with my own eyes, and of course, I believe it," replied Emperor Wen-tsung.

"You owe this belief to Kuan-yin, who has expounded the Dharma to you by her appearance in the shell," declared the Master.

Master Wei-cheng's explanation is very skillful. Such wisdom originates from the mind of Ch'an. When one has the Ch'an mind, anything one says would be profound. If we can understand and realize the Dharma through our personal experiences, everything in the world will reveal the Buddha-truth to us. Green willows and luxuriant yellow flowers will all become the spiritual body of the *Tathāgata*. The sounds of waves in the ocean and rain drops from eaves will become the sounds of the *Tathāgata* expounding the Dharma. In that case, why is it necessary for bodhisattvas to transform themselves into physical bodies of human beings to explain the Dharma?

Hearing and Not Hearing

When Ch'an Master Ch'ing-lin Shi-ch'ien met Master Tung-shan for the first time, the latter asked him, "From where did you come?"

"Wuling," answered Ch'ing-lin.

"What's the difference between the Dharma there and the Dharma here?" inquired Tung-shan again.

"The Dharma there is like a flower blossoming in the desert."

Upon hearing this, Master Tung-shan told his attendants, "Prepare some good food for him," but Ch'ing-lin left scornfully.

Tung-shan said to those present, "This master will soon become a teacher whom all novices would like to follow."

One day, Master Ch'ing-lin went to bid farewell to Tung-shan.

"Where are you going?" T'ung-shan asked him.

Ch'ing-lin answered, "The sun can't hide itself from us because being the sun, it's bound to cast its rays everywhere on Earth."

Tung-shan approved of what Ch'ing-lin had said and saw him off to the monastery gate by saying, "Take good care of yourself."

They were about to say goodbye to each other when Tung-shan suddenly asked, "Can you summarize your feelings about this trip in one sentence?"

Without thinking, Ch'ing-lin said, "Although every step I take will be on the earth, I will not cast any shadow."

When he heard this, Tung-shan became lost in thought. After a while, Ch'ing-lin asked, "Master, why are you not saying anything?"

Tung-shan asked in response, "I've said so much to you. Why do you accuse me of not saying anything?"

Kneeling down, Ch'ing-lin said, "Master, I didn't hear what you said, but I heard what you didn't say."

Helping Ch'ing-lin up, Tung-shan said, "Please go. You may now go to the place where there are neither words nor instruction."

Ch'an masters are very honest. They are not lying when they claim that they do not hear what others say, or they hear what others do not say. What is implied here is that if one can hear the silent, wordless expounding of the Dharma, one is sure to hear the sound of Truth.

Drying Mushrooms in the Sun

There was an eighty year-old hunchbacked monk who lived in Eihei Temple in Japan. While he was drying mushrooms in the sun one day, Zen Master Dōgen, who is the Abbot of Eihei Temple, saw him and said, "Venerable Master, why are you still working so hard at your advanced age? Please take a rest. I can have somebody do this for you."

The senior monk said, "But that somebody isn't I."

"You're right. At least you don't have to work under the scorching sun," argued Dōgen.

"Do you mean I should wait until it's cloudy or raining to dry the mushrooms?" retorted the monk.

Being the Abbot of Eihei Temple, Master Dōgen issued instruc-

tions to everyone there. Yet, in the presence of this old monk, he had
to surrender his authority.

**Ch'an practitioners do not ask others to do anything for them, nor
do they put off anything for tomorrow if it could be done today.
"Until when should I wait, if I don't do it now?" is a question
people in the modern world should ask themselves.**

What Do You Eat Everyday?

Ch'an Master Yün-chü Tao-ying made a special trip to meet Master
Tung-shan Liang-chieh. The latter asked, "From where did you come?"

"I came from Ch'an Master Ts'ui-wei," answered Tao-ying.

"What did he teach you?" Liang-chieh inquired.

Tao-ying replied, "Every year, we make offerings to the sixteen
and five hundred *arhans* during the first month of the lunar year. The
memorial ceremony is always grand. Once, I asked Master Ts'ui-wei,
'We make offerings to the *arhans* with such a solemn ceremony. Do
you think that they'll come to accept them?' The Master only said,
'What do you eat every day?' I think that this was his instruction."

Liang-chieh was surprised to hear this and asked, "Are you sure
this was what Ts'ui-wei taught you?"

"Yes," Tao-ying asserted.

Liang-chieh was pleased and praised Master Ts'ui-wei. Afterward,
Tao-ying asked him, "Master, what do you eat every day if I may ask?"

Without thinking, Liang-chieh replied, "I eat and drink all day
long, but I've never eaten a grain of rice, nor have I drunk a single drop
of water."

After hearing this, Tao-ying clapped his hands and said, "Master,
you really eat rice and drink water everyday."

**Confucius once said, "Make offerings to celestial beings as if they
were present." Whether the spirits of heaven will come to accept
the offerings is not important. What is important is that we,
ourselves, have come to accept them. If you are asked about what
you eat every day, the answer is that what you eat is not really**

eating. Eating and not eating are only questions of arising and ceasing, respectively. If we are able to eat without eating and also are able to not eat while eating, then we have transformed ourselves from the conditioned state into the unconditioned state, from form into no form, from arising and ceasing into transcendence of both arising and ceasing. If we can do all of this, our daily consumption actually represents our gradual liberation from all attachments.

The Fallen Head

Once, Ch'an Master Lung-ya said to Master Tê-shan, "If I were holding a very sharp sword and were ready to chop off your head now, what would you do?"

Tê-shan took a few steps forward, stretched out his neck, and replied, "Cut my head off."

Lung-ya laughed heartily and said, "Your head has already fallen on the ground."

With a loud laugh, Tê-shan said, "Yes, it has fallen already."

Later, when Lung-ya studied under the guidance of Master Tung-shan Liang-chieh, he told the Master how he had chopped off Tê-shan's head. Tung-shan asked, "What did Tê-shan say after he had been beheaded?"

"He laughed with me and agreed that his head had fallen already," answered Lung-ya.

Upon hearing this, Tung-shan corrected him, "You should not have said that you chopped off Tê-shan's head. In fact, you were beheaded by Tê-shan."

Lung-ya argued, "But Master, my head is still on my neck. How can you say that it was chopped off?"

Tung-shan burst into laughter and then explained, "Tê-shan has beheaded you, and you have shown it to me in person."

What Master Tung-shan said was like earthshaking thunder to Lung-ya. Lung-ya finally was awakened and became enlightened.

Lung-ya's intention to chop off Tê-shan's head implied that he did not forget about others. The starting point of this intention was his self-ego. Master Tung-shan reminded Lung-ya of chopping off his own head so that he may be free from his attachment to his self-ego.

"To chop off one's own head and show it to others" is not an illusion. It indicates that while Ch'an believes in the emptiness of all material matters, it does not negate them. Therefore, as soon as one harmonizes the self-ego and with the ego of others, one will surely attain enlightenment.

Spitting

One day, Ch'an Master Ma-tsu Tao-i was sitting in meditation. Suddenly, he felt like spitting, so he spat on the statue of the Buddha. His attendant was astonished by his behavior and asked, "Master, why did you spit on the statue?"

Ma-tsu immediately let out two dry coughs, then asked in reply, "The Buddha's true body exists everywhere in the universe. I need to spit again. Can you tell me where I should spit?"

The attendant was at a loss for words.

Another time, Master Ma-tsu angrily spat into the air. Not understanding the significance of this action either, the attendant asked, "Master, why were you mad when you spat just now?"

Ma-tsu explained, "Well, when I was sitting in meditation, mountains, rivers, and a profusion of things under the sun appeared in my mind. I was fed up with all of this, therefore I couldn't help spitting."

This statement confused the attendant even more. "But Master, what you saw in your meditation was the auspicious sign of your successful self-cultivation. Why didn't you like it?"

"It's something good for you. However, I'm fed up with it."

The attendant stared blankly at him and asked, "Master, what state of mind is this?"

"The bodhisattvas' state of mind!" replied Ma-tsu.

Shaking his head and with his eye brows knit, the attendant declared, "It's really difficult for me to understand this state of mind."

"Because you're not a bodhisattva. You're only a human being."

"But doesn't a bodhisattva mean an enlightened sentient being?" asked the attendant.

Upon hearing this, Ma-tsu reprimanded him, "You're a fool with no spiritual insight. How can you claim to be a sentient being who is enlightened?"

With the help of Ma-tsu, the attendant attained some realization.

Average people respect statues of the Buddha without knowing the Buddha. Since the empty space is filled with the Dharma-body, Ma-tsu indicated that he had realized this fact by spitting on the statue.

Furthermore, most people hope to visualize auspicious signs to increase their confidence while sitting in meditation. Ma-tsu dislikes such signs, demonstrating that he has attained the realm in which all differences in the universe are exterminated, while equality and harmonization prevail. In contrast, the attendant rigidly adheres to worldly views. No wonder Ma-tsu reprimands the attendant!

Where Shall I Go?

One day, Ch'an Master Tung-shan went to see a novice by the name of Tê-chao who was very ill. When the Master arrived, the novice implored, "Oh, Master! Please be compassionate and save me? I've been seeking the Dharma earnestly. Can you bear to see your disciple die unenlightened?"

"Whose child are you?" asked Tung-shan.

"I'm a son of someone without the Buddha-nature."

Looking at the novice intently, Tung-shan was deep in thought.

Tê-chao grew impatient and asked anxiously, "Master, when mountains on all sides are pressing toward me, what should I do?"

The Master replied, "I also used to walk under others' eaves."

Tê-chao asked, "Master, if you and I met under the same eaves, should we avoid each other or not?"

"We shouldn't," said the Master.

"If we shouldn't avoid each other, where do you want me to go?"

"Since the five modes of existence, the six directions of reincarnation, and the ten Dharma-worlds[46] exist, there are roads everywhere.

Why do you have to worry about it? If you can't rest assured, you may go and grow rice in the cultivated fields!" Tung-shan instructed.

Upon hearing this, Tê-chao said, "Master, please take care." He then sank into his chair with a blank look in his eyes and passed away.

Tung-shan shook his staff in front of the young novice three times, saying, "Although you're able to depart this way, you will not be able to return the same way."

Although Tê-chao was dying, he was still searching for the Path beyond life and death. He did not know what to do when birth, old age, sickness, and death were pressing on toward him like four mountains. Master Tung-shan pointed out to him that there were paths everywhere. This does not mean that just anybody can find the right road. To cultivate the land and grow rice merits the attention of every Buddhist. Tê-chao passed away peacefully, implying that he had found his way out. However, Master Tung-shan did not think that the novice could return the same way, implying that it would not be easy even for Ch'an practitioners to be reborn the way that they choose.

Climbing a Mountain

One day, Ch'an Master Tung-shan said to Master Yün-chü, "You should have been practicing hard in the meditation hall. Where have you been?"

"I have been climbing a mountain," answered Yün-chü.

"Which one did you climb?" continued Tung-shan.

"There's none worth climbing!" declared Yün-chü.

"Do you mean you've climbed all the mountains already?" Tung-shan asked.

"No, not really," Yün-chü replied.

"But you had to find a way out," Tung-shan continued.

"There is no way out," answered Yün-chü.

"But if you had not found a way out, how were you able to meet me?" Tung-shan asked.

"If I had found a way out, you and I would have lived on two different sides of the mountain," answered Yün-chü.

Another time, Tung-shan asked Yün-chü again, "Where have you been?"

"I've been climbing a mountain," replied the latter.

"Did you go to the top?" Tung-shan inquired.

"Yes," answered Yün-chü straightforwardly.

"Did you see other people there?" inquired Tung-shan.

"No, I didn't," Yün-chü answered honestly.

"This shows that you didn't climb to the top," scoffed Tung-shan.

"If I hadn't been to the top, how would I know that no one was there?" Yün-chü countered.

"Why didn't you stay there for a while?" Tung-shan insisted.

"It's not that I didn't want to stay. Only the people there wouldn't let me stay."

While laughing heartily, Tung-shan remarked, "For a long time, I suspected that you have already been to the mountain."

When asked if there were people at the top of the mountain, Yün-chü first said, "No." Later he said that the people there would not allow him to stay. Weren't these responses contradictory? No, they weren't. For the real ego does not exist in the mountain of the five aggregates—the five components of a human being, nor is the ego allowed to stay there permanently.

In the eyes of an unilluminated person, having and not having or existence and nonexistence are separate entities; yet, for Ch'an Buddhists, they are not opposites. They are simply two aspects of one thing. Thus, if one can integrate the two and find the middle path between them, one will obtain the wisdom of Ch'an.

Porridge and Tea

Ch'an Master Chao-chou devoted much of his attention to Buddhism in an everyday context. He displayed the charisma of a Ch'an master in his day-to-day activities. Once, a group of novices went to seek instruction from him. One novice respectfully requested, "Master, I've just entered monastic training. Please instruct me."

Chao-chou asked in reply, "Have you had your porridge yet?"

"Yes," answered the student.

"Go and wash your bowl!" instructed Chao-chou.

The first novice thus attained realization. Then the second one went and said, "Master, I've just entered monastic training. Please be compassionate and teach me." Instead of responding to his request, Chao-chou asked, "How long have you been here?"

"I have just arrived here today," replied the second novice.

"Have you had tea?" Chao-chou asked again.

"Yes," he replied.

"Then go and register in the assembly hall!" instructed the Master.

Having studied in this monastery for more than ten years, the third novice was different from the first two. He said to Chao-chou, "Master, I've been here for over a decade. Since I've never had the honor of obtaining instruction and guidance from you, I would like to take leave of you and study elsewhere."

Pretending to be surprised, Chao-chou complained, "That's unfair of you. Ever since you came here, I have drunk the tea that you brought me each time. Whenever you offered me food, I ate it. Each time you greeted me with your palms together, I lowered my eyes. Whenever you prostrated yourself at my feet to pay me homage, I nodded my head in response. I've given you my instruction on everything. How could you say such a terrible thing about me?"

After hearing this, the third novice was thinking hard about what Chao-chou had said to him. Then, the Master interrupted, "It's enough if you've understood what I said. Don't try to reason with your mind because thought is characterized by notions of differentiation. It will lead you astray from the right Path to the Dharma."

Although he seemed to understand, the novice still asked, "How can I always stay on the right Path?"

Chao-chou observed, "To liberate yourself from the unenlightened mind, there is no other holy way—if one is unattached to deluding conditions, one will instantaneously attain enlightenment."

Neither the Dharma nor the mind of Ch'an is divorced from daily life. Thus, having tasty food is Ch'an, and so is sleeping peacefully. The Dharma will become useless if it is separated from life. Today, many practitioners concentrate their attention on the question of birth and death but ignore daily life. They are actually far from the right Path that is leading to the Truth.

The Monk in the Body of a Wild Fox

Ch'an Master Pai-chang Huai-hai was the successor to Master Ma-tsu Tao-i. In the Ch'an School, there is a saying: "Ma-tsu built the monastery, while Pai-chang laid down the regulations." This statement emphasizes the latter's contribution.

One day, Pai-chang expounded the Dharma in the preaching hall. After he finished, everyone in the audience left except for an old monk. Pai-chang asked, "Who is standing over there?"

The monk answered, "I'm not a man. I'm actually a wild fox. Many years ago, I meditated here on Pai-chang Shan. Once, a novice asked me, 'Are great Buddhist practitioners still subject to the law of cause and effect?' I told him 'No. They are not subject to the law of cause and effect.' Because of that response, I was reborn as a fox and have remained so for five hundred lifetimes. Master, I would like to ask you to answer 'the question' for me today, so that I won't ever be reborn as a fox again."

Upon hearing this, Master Pai-chang said compassionately, "Please ask 'the question.'"

"Are great Buddhist practitioners still subject to the law of cause and effect?"

"They cannot ignore the law of cause and effect!" exclaimed Pai-chang.

The old monk became enlightened instantaneously. Joining his palms together in front of his chest, he prostrated and said good-bye. The next day, Pai-chang took all the clergies from the monastery to a cave in the mountain, where they found a dead fox. Pai-chang told his disciples to cremate it with the same ceremony as would be performed for clergies who have passed away.

This is a famous *kung-an* in the Ch'an School. Because of the phrase "not subject to the law of cause and effect," the old monk had remained in the body of a fox for five hundred lifetimes. When Master Pai-chang changed "not subject to the law of cause and effect" to "cannot ignore the law of cause and effect," the monk's long suffering ended. Why should the two phrases make such a world of difference? The reason may have been that cause and effect in the moral realm have their corresponding relations. "Not

subject to the law of cause and effect" has the implication that a Buddhist practitioner's life is not governed by the relations, and hence deny all moral responsibilities of Buddhist practitioners. Such an answer would be considered irresponsible and wrong. Since nobody could dwell outside the law of cause and effect, the statement "They cannot ignore the law of cause and effect" implies that all monastics who practice meditation for the attainment of enlightenment should be aware of these relationships.

Does a Dog Have the Buddha-nature?

Chao-chou Ts'ung-shên was a very humorous Ch'an master and enjoyed the reputation of being "Chao-chou the ancient Buddha." Once he was asked, "What is Chao-chou?"

He replied, "It is the gate in each of the four directions—north, south, east, and west." This answer had a double meaning. If the questioner had the town Chaochou in mind, the reference to the four gates of the four city walls would be the best answer to the question. If he was really being asked to describe himself, the four gates would symbolize his Buddhist style, which was vivacious, free, and easy, with openings in all directions for easy access.

On another occasion, a novice monk asked him, "Does a dog have the Buddha-nature?"

Without thinking, Chao-chou replied, "No."

The novice was not convinced, "All beings, up to Buddhas and down to mole crickets and ants, have the Buddha-nature. Why doesn't a dog have it?"

"Because it has 'karma-consciousness[47],'" replied the Master.

However, when another novice asked him whether a dog had the Buddha-nature, he answered, "Yes."

This novice was not convinced either, arguing, "If it does, why did it come into this world in the dog's vile skin bag?"

Chao-chou explained, "It chose to do so."

In this well-known *kung-an*, Chao-chou gave two different answers to the same question, because "having" and "not having" possess the same implication for Ch'an masters. They are two aspects of one thing and therefore should not be separated, nor should they be defined as two different words. The *Heart Sutra*[48] states: "Those who realize the immaterial, universal reality behind all phenomena would become bodhisattvas."

A considerable effort is required in distinguishing "having" from "not having" because the difference is impossible to explain through words. It is just like a mute person having a dream; he or she cannot tell others about it. Only when one is free from worldly desires and passions will one be able to understand the relationship.

Unilluminated people hold that a contradiction always exists between "having" and "not having," right and wrong, or good and evil. For this reason, they cannot find the Path to behold their own Buddha-nature. "Does a dog have the Buddha-nature?" This nature cannot be described in terms of "having" or "not having" in the first place. Since Chao-chou was asked such a question, he had no other alternative but to give the affirmative and negative answers.

I Do Not Have Time to Get Old

Ch'an Master Fo-kuang had a disciple, Ta-chih, who had traveled and studied Buddhism in other places for twenty years. One day, Ta-chih returned and reported what he had learned to Master Fo-kuang in the preaching hall. Fo-kuang listened attentively with a smile to comfort and encourage him. After he had finished, Ta-chih asked, "Master, how has everything been with you for the last twenty years?"

Fo-kuang replied, "Very well. I've been teaching, expounding the Dharma, writing books, and compiling sutras. In other words, I've been swimming in the sea of the Buddha-truth. No one in this world lives a more joyful life than I do. I'm happy with what I do each day."

Concerned, Ta-chih said, "Master, you should get more rest."

Since it was already very late at night, Fo-kuang concluded the conversation by saying, "You should rest now. Let's continue our talk later, since we will be spending a lot of time together."

Early next morning, while Ta-chih was still in bed, he faintly heard Master Fo-kuang chanting the sutras in his room. During the day, the

Master was busy explaining the Dharma to numerous groups of Buddhists who visited the temple. When they left, he commented on the reports of the novices and prepared teaching materials for lay Buddhists. It seemed that he had much more work to do during a day than any one individual could handle.

At one point, as Fo-kuang finished talking to some Buddhists, Ta-chih seized this rare opportunity to ask, "Master, we've been away from each other for twenty years, but you're still living such a busy life. Why is it that you don't feel old?"

Fo-kuang replied, "Because I do not have time to get old."

Afterward, these words continued to ring in Ta-chih's ears.

There are young people in our society who already feel old because there is a decline in their will-power. On the other hand, there are elders in our society who still feel energetic and vigorous.

"Having no time to feel old" actually has the implication of having no concept of being old. Confucius once said, "If one is so immersed in work as to forget one's meals and is so joyful without anxieties, one will not feel that one is aging." This also describes the Ch'an master's outlook on life.

There once was an old man. When someone asked about his age, he replied that he was four years old. The people who posed the question were surprised by his response. He explained, "In the first seventy years of my life, I lived for myself. That kind of selfish life was meaningless. In the past four years, I've learned to do something for humanity. Therefore, I've lived a more meaningful life. This is why I say that I'm only four years old."

Who Knows You?

A nun once asked Ch'an Master Lung-t'an, "How should I cultivate myself so that I may be reborn as a male in my next life?"

"How long have you been a nun?" asked Lung-t'an.

"This question concerns my past," replied the nun. "What has it got to do with my future? I just want to know if I'll be able to be reborn as a male someday."

"What are you now?" Lung-t'an asked.

Surprised, the nun asked, "I'm a female. Can't you see that?"

"You're a female, but who can see that?" the Master replied.

After hearing this, the nun began to realize the error underlying her question.

The difference between male and female is superficial. Since the Buddha-nature within all beings is the same, there is no real difference between male and female. Because many of us are misled by the different appearance of gender, we fail to recognize our identical Buddha-nature. Also, this nature cannot be seen. It can only be realized through self-cultivation and personal experience.

Unable to Get Back the True Mind

There was once a Buddhist named Chu Tz'u-mu, who was very good in the practice of Pure Land teaching. One day, he made a special trip to consult Master Fo-kuang. "Master," he said, "I've been chanting and devoutly paying homage to the Buddha for more than twenty years. Recently, when I chant the name of the Buddha, a mysterious feeling arises."

"How do you feel?" asked Fo-kuang.

"In the past, when I chanted the Buddha's name, I beheld the Buddha-nature within myself. Even if I chanted to myself, I could hear the Buddha's name, and if I didn't want to chant, the Buddha's name would continue to ring in my ears."

"That's wonderful!" Fo-kuang said with approval, "It shows that you've chanted your way into the stage of continuous pure thoughts and your mind is in harmony with the Buddha's. You've found your true mind."

Chu Tz'u-mu hastened to correct the Master by saying, "Thank you. But I am not experiencing this any more. I'm very upset because I've lost my true mind."

"How could you do that?" asked Fo-kuang.

Chu Tz'u-mu answered, "Because my mind is no longer in harmony with the Buddha's. Therefore, the continuous pure thoughts and the Buddha's preaching sounds have all disappeared. I can't find them any more. Oh, Master! I feel so awful about this. Please tell me where I can find what I've lost."

Fo-kuang instructed Chu Tz'u-mu, "If you want to find your true mind, you should know that it's not anywhere else but within yourself."

"Could you be more specific?" asked Chu.

"Your true mind has left you because unenlightened thoughts have unlocked your false mind," answered the Master.

Upon hearing this, Chu seemed to have attained some realization.

Losing one's true mind is just like losing oneself or failing to find one's own home. How can people be misled? This is because their true minds are shrouded by false desires and sensations.

A Whisk Expounding the Dharma

When Ch'an Master Tung-shan Liang-chieh was studying under the guidance of Master Kuei-shan Ling-yu, he once asked, "Master, I don't understand Master Nan-yang Hui-chung's *kung-an* 'Non-Sentient Beings Expound the Dharma.' It's generally accepted that sentient beings expound the Dharma. How can non-sentient beings do the same? For example, how can we expect tables, chairs, and stools to expound the Dharma? Could you explain this to me?"

Kuei-shan raised the whisk in his hand and asked, "Do you understand this?"

"No, I don't. Please be compassionate and teach me."

However, Kuei-shan countered, "My mouth, which was given to me by my parents, will never tell you the secret of 'this.'"

Tung-shan objected to the answer, "Are you saying there's a secret in the Dharma?"

Lifting the whisk again, Kuei-shan said decisively, "This is the secret!"

"Well," Tung-shan said, "if you're not going to tell me the secret, I'll go and ask other Ch'an masters who had previously studied with you."

Kuei-shan did not have any objections. "That's fine with me. I suggest you go to Yuhsien County in Liling. Monk Yün-yen resides in one of the caves there. If you can find him, he will surely answer your question."

Tung-shan immediately asked, "What kind of a person is he?"

"He used to be a disciple of mine," replied Wei-shan.

"What did he want to learn from you?" Tung-shan continued.

"He wanted to know the most effective way in the eradication of defilements."

"What did you tell him?" Tung-shan asked pointedly.

"I told him that the most effective way was to conform to his teacher's instructions," answered Kuei-shan.

"Did he do that?" asked Tung-shan curiously.

"Yes," Kuei-shan affirmed. "He conformed to my instructions very well. He understood how the inanimate objects could expound the Dharma. Do you see that the whisk is expounding the Dharma now?"

After hearing this, Tung-shan became enlightened.

It is true that a whisk can expound the Dharma. For example, with some people, holding the whisk erect is a symbol of human dignity, while bending the whisk symbolizes that everything should start from their basis.

The Dharma is the Truth. How can the Truth be expounded clearly? Expositions will not add anything. Without them, truth will not lose anything either. Even if one gives an extravagant account of it, truth remains the same. It states in the sutras that the Buddha's teaching is like a raft for crossing a river. Once one has crossed the river, one ought to leave the raft behind. Even the Buddha's teaching, which is the Dharma, should be abandoned.

I Want Your Eyes

One day, Ch'an Master Yün-yen was weaving straw sandals when Master Tung-shan passed by.

Tung-shan said, "Master, may I have something from you?"

"Tell me, what do you want?" inquired Yün-yen.

"I want your eyes," Tung-shan said bluntly.

Yün-yen asked calmly, "My eyes? What has happened to yours?"

"I don't have any," answered Tung-shan.

With a faint smile, Yün-yen asked, "If you had eyes, what would you do with them?"

Tung-shan could not arrive at a response.

Master Yün-yen then said in all earnestness, "I think what you actually want are your own eyes, not mine."

Tung-shan now corrected himself, "In fact, I don't want any eyes."

Master Yün-yen could no longer tolerate his statements which are contradictory and shouted, "Get out!"

Tung-shan was not frightened but said, "I don't mind getting out, but I don't have eyes and thus can't see the road before me."

Yün-yen touched his own heart with his hand and said, "Didn't I give this to you a long time ago? Why do you still say that you can't see?"

When he heard this, Tung-shan finally attained realization.

It was strange for Tung-shan to ask for another person's eyes. Even the brilliant Master Yün-yen could just tell him that his eyes were on his own face, and so he did not need to ask for any. Only when he realized that what Tung-shan wanted was not the eyes on his face could Yün-yen point out to him his mind's eye. This, in turn, enlightened Tung-shan.

Eyes are for seeing earthly phenomena. However, this observation is superficial and has both a beginning and an end. Only the mental vision can behold the essence of all phenomena. This kind of observation is universal and absolute. Although Tung-shan had eyes, he could not see the road, which is his own Buddha-nature, leading to his goal of becoming a Buddha. Only when Master Yün-yen imparted to him the wonderful use of the eye of the mind did he attain realization.

Not in Other Places

Once, Ch'an Master Tung-shan Liang-chieh asked Master Yün-yen, "Master! If someone asks me to describe your appearance after you pass away, what should I say?"

"Tell the person that I will not be in other places," answered Yün-yen.

Upon hearing this, Tung-shan immersed in deep thought.

Yün-yen continued, "Master Liang-chieh, you ought to be very careful with the way you handle such an issue."

Tung-shan was still baffled. He could not see why Master Yün-yen reminded him of this and wondered if he had violated any rule by asking the question.

Only later, when he saw his own reflection in a river did Tung-shan suddenly understand what Yün-yen meant. Hence, he wrote:

> Guard against searching in other places;
> Otherwise, you will become ever further
>   estranged from yourself.
> When I strolled along the water today,
> I found myself mirrored in it every time I
>   looked.
> The reflection was me;
> But I was not the reflection.
> With this self-attained realization,
> My mind has merged with my teacher's.

Tung-shan went back to Yün-yen and said, "Master! I'll always know your appearance and charm in the future, even after aeons."

"But I won't exist then," answered Master Yün-yen.

Tung-shan hastened to repeat, "No, you will be neither in other places nor other times."

How should the appearances and charms of monastics be described after they pass away? If they can be depicted, they must be false images. Since looks and charms are impermanent and phenomenal, how can they be mistaken for the true nature? In other words, the real appearance of a Ch'an practitioner is beyond description. It cannot be found in other places nor at any specific time because it transcends time and space. The explanation for this is that the Buddha-nature does not have form, yet, at the same time, it appears in all forms.

Not Being Separated for a Second

Ch'an Master Tung-shan went to bid farewell to Master Yün-yen. "Where are you going?" asked the latter.

Tung-shan answered, "I just want to change my surrounding in which I study Ch'an. Being alone, I'll wander far and wide and beg for my food. As for my destination, I still don't know where I'm going."

"Aren't you planning to go to Hunan?" Yün-yen suggested.

Without any hesitation, Tung-shan answered, "No."

"Then, you must be going home," concluded Yün-yen.

"No," replied Tung-shan.

Seeing that he was getting nowhere, Master Yün-yen changed the subject, "When are you planning to return?"

Tung-shan replied, "I'll return as soon as I find a place to stay."

Yün-yen knew that Tung-shan had already decided to leave. If he continued to quibble over the question of coming and going, he was afraid that Tung-shan might feel that his knowledge still remained at the level of differentiation. Therefore, he exclaimed passionately as if he were revealing the essence of life, "The Dharma-realm is vast. Once you leave here, it would be very difficult for us to meet again."

Joining his palms together in front of his chest, Tung-shan replied, "Although standing across from each other, we've actually never faced each other. On the other hand, even if we are away from each other for countless ages, we won't be separated, not even for a second." After saying this, Tung-shan promptly left. Master Yün-yen silently watched his figure disappear over the endless horizon.

While it is common for disciples to take leave of their masters and study in other places, it would be very unusual for them to leave without having any idea of where they are going. Tung-shan Liang-chieh had stayed with Master Yün-yen for several decades. His departure is actually a sign of his search for a place to settle down. Such a place is the realm of nirvana. This explains why Master Yün-yen said, "Once you leave here, it would be very difficult for us to meet again."

Irreplaceable

Before Master Lin-chi passed away, he instructed his disciples, "After I die, you shouldn't let the Dharma die with me!"

Ch'an Master San-sheng Hui-jan immediately said, "We're your disciples. How could we dare do anything like that?"

Upon hearing this, Lin-chi said, "If you're asked to explain the way to enlightenment, what will you say?"

Hui-jan quickly cried out, as Master Lin-chi often did when he was teaching his students.

Nevertheless, Master Lin-chi was not pleased with the response. He sighed, "I've never expected the Buddha's doctrines to die in the shouts of my disciples. How can I stop feeling heartbroken now that I see this is going to happen?" With these words, he passed away while sitting upright in his chair.

Master Hui-jan was confused, "Our master had always given a loud shout to his visitors. Why can't we imitate him and let out a cry?"

Just as he had finished speaking, Master Lin-chi suddenly came back to life and replied, "If I ate, I would be the one who would feel satiated. When I die, none of you can take my place."

Hui-jan prostrated himself and said, "Please forgive me, Master. Please go on living with us and teach us some more."

Giving a loud shout, Lin-chi said, "I won't let you imitate me!" After saying this, he passed away.

Ch'an practitioners dislike being imitated more than anything else because a mechanical copy can never resemble the original. Ch'an masters vary in their methods of instructing students. Huang-po used his monk's staff; Lin-chi shouted; Chao-chou served tea; and Yün-men offered cakes. From the examples provided, none of them could be imitated successfully. Ch'an practitioners should be able to live their lives independently.

Required Courses of Action

Ch'an Master Wu-tê had a novice by the name of Yüan-ch'ih. Although this novice had studied diligently, he still could neither understand nor master the essence of Ch'an. Therefore, at one particular evening assembly, he asked Master Wu-tê, "I've been at the monastery for many years. Still, I'm ignorant of most concepts of the Ch'an School. I feel that I'm wasting the offerings given by the faithful each day, because I have not been awakened yet. Therefore, I would like to ask the Master to have compassion on me and tell me besides meditation and cultivation through labor, what other courses of action should I take."

Wu-tê replied, "You had better look after your two vultures, two deer, and two hawks. You also have to restrain the worm in your mouth. At the same time, you need to struggle continuously with a bear and take care of a sick person. If you can do all that conscientiously, you'll be greatly benefitted."

Yüan-ch'ih was very much bewildered by what Wu-tê said. "Master, I'm all alone in this world. I didn't bring animals such as vultures, deer, or hawks, with me when I came here. How can I look after things I don't even have? Furthermore, what I'm interested in is the proper courses of action that will help me to understand Ch'an better. What does this have to do with those animals you spoke of?"

Smiling, Wu-tê explained, "By the two vultures, I mean your eyes, on which you should often keep a close watch. The two deer are your feet that need to be steered, so they won't go astray. The two hawks refer to your hands, which should work diligently to fulfill their obligations. By the worm in your mouth, I mean your tongue which should be bound tightly. The bear is your heart. You'll have to restrain its selfish intentions and individualism. To put all this in the words of Confucius, you shouldn't look at, do, think, touch, or say things that violate Buddhist ethics. As for the sick person, it's your body. You shouldn't let it sink into evil. I believe these are indispensable courses of action one should take for self-cultivation."

In the sutras, the six sense organs—eyes, ears, nose, tongue, body, and mind—are described as an uninhabited village, which is captured by six bandits. They cling to the six dusts every day and

do evil things. The six sense organs are just like tigers, jackals, and wolves, or like vultures, hawks, and poisonous snakes. If they are carefully watched, they may avoid touching, doing, saying, or looking at things that violate Buddhist ethics. Here, we can perceive the harmonization of Buddhism and Confucianism.

Returning from Death

Once, Ch'an Master Nan-ch'üan P'u-yüan was sitting in meditation. Suddenly, he let out a loud cry that startled his attendant. The latter went over hurriedly to see if anything was wrong with his master. But Nan-ch'üan said, "Go to the sanitarium and see if anybody has just passed away."

On his way there, the attendant ran into the head monk of the sanitarium. The two went to report to Master Nan-ch'üan: "A roving monk has just died."

They had barely finished speaking when a monk, who was in charge of the reception, approached and said to the Master, "The dead monk has returned from death."

"How is he now?" asked Nan-ch'üan.

"He wants to see you. However, he is a monk who neither cultivates goodness nor makes friends with anyone."

Nan-ch'üan went to see the sick monk in the sanitarium. When he arrived, he asked, "Where were you just now?"

"I was in the nether world," answered the monk.

"What did you do there?" continued the Master.

The monk then described his experience, "It seemed as if I had walked about one hundred miles. Both my feet and hands were in pain, and I was very thirsty; I had to stop. Suddenly, someone appeared and invited me into a big building. Since I was very tired, I wanted to go in and have a rest. While I was walking up the staircase, I met an old monk. He wouldn't let me pass and shouted angrily at me instead. I was so frightened that I leaned back and fell off the stairs. Thus, I've received this chance to see you again, Master."

Nan-ch'üan scolded him, "What a splendid building that was! Since you haven't accumulated enough merits, you could not go in. You are fortunate to have met the old monk. Otherwise, you might have fallen into hell." From then on, the sick monk cultivated goodness day and night. He lived until he was over seventy years old and died peacefully. Everyone called him "the monk enlightened by Nan-ch'üan."

In his intense contemplation, Master Nan-ch'üan could go up to heaven or down to hell. He could also let out a loud cry to bring somebody who was dead back to this world. Ch'an masters often are said to ignore human feelings, however, Nan-ch'üan cared so much about his disciple that he gave him a rare chance to relive his life. According to a Chinese saying: "A prodigal who returns is more precious than gold."

Who Is More Important?

One day, a devotee went to the temple to pay homage to the Buddha. Afterward, he went to the reception hall for a rest. He had just sat down when he heard a young monk in charge of receiving guests tell the elderly Ch'an Master Wu-tê, "Please bring some tea for our guest."

A few seconds later, the devotee heard the monk call out again, "Master, there is too much incense ash on the altar. Please wipe it away . . . don't forget to water the flowers . . . don't forget to ask our guests to stay for lunch . . ."

The devotee felt sorry for Wu-tê and could not bear to see the young monk ordering the senior master around. He thus went up to Wu-tê and asked, "Master, who is this young monk?"

"He's a disciple of mine," replied the Master proudly.

Hardly able to believe what he had just heard, the devotee asked, "But if he's your disciple, why doesn't he show any respect for you? Why does he tell you to do all these things?"

The Master answered gratefully, "I'm fortunate to have such a capable disciple. When devotees come to make offerings to the Buddha, he only asks me to serve them tea instead of speaking to them. He replaces incense and puts offerings on the altar everyday, while I just wipe off the dust. He only wants me to tell our guests to stay for meals; he doesn't ask me to cook or make tea. He arranges everything in the monastery, and he has saved me much hard work."

The devotee still was not sure if he understood the Master and asked suspiciously, "Who is more important here, senior monastics or novices?"

Master Wu-tê answered, "Of course, the seniors, but the novices are useful as well."

Normally, devotees support and protect senior clergies rather than the younger ones. They make offerings to the former instead of the latter. In the minds of devotees, senior clergies are more important. These devotees fail to see that young novices may become great masters just as princes may become kings.

Master Wu-tê did not underestimate his disciples. He was able to see this relationship from a different angle, and thus, he was content with the situation in his monastery. This reflects the concept of equality within Ch'an.

NOTES

1. To inherit the robe and bowl means to become the successor in the line of Ch'an patriarchs, which began with Bodhidharma, who was considered to be the first patriarch in China and the twenty-eighth patriarch in the line tracing back to Buddha's disciple, Mahākāśyapa.

2. The thief of the mind is what gives rise to our delusions and ignorance.

3. The six roots are the six sense organs as recognized by Buddhism; they are our eyes, ears, nose, tongue, body, and mind.

4. Rahula, the son of the Buddha, became a disciple of the Buddha at seven, and thus, he is considered the patron of novices.

5. The eternal refers to that which is not subject to conditioned co-production and exists outside of time.

6. True nature implies the embodiment of Truth, the absolute.

7. No-mind implies mindless, without thought, the real, immaterial mind that is free of illusion.

8. The sutras were periodically laid out in the sun to prevent damage from the moisture prevalent in the humid mountain areas, where many monasteries and nunneries were located.

9. Tathāgata's Ch'an refers to the kind of contemplative practice that was taught by the Buddha.

10. Patriarchs' Ch'an was introduced in China by Bodhidharma, who was the first patriarch. Its basis of teaching is beyond any doctrines and not relying on any written or verbal communication. Ch'an is transmitted directly from the mind of the master to the mind of the student. Patriarchs' Ch'an is the attainment of Buddhahood whereby the individual seeks one's own nature.

11. It was a common practice for Ch'an masters to adopt the name of the place where they were from as the first two words of their name. Since Master Ta-t'ung was from T'ou-tzu Shan, his name became

T'ou-tzu Ta-t'ung, and he might also be referred to as either T'ou-tzu
or Ta-t'ung.

12. Hsin-lo was one of the three kingdoms of ancient Korea.

13. Individual monks and nuns are restricted to owning three robes,
according to the rules of the *Sangha*. When Buddhism was introduced
to various countries, certain modifications were made to these rules due
to differing climatic and cultural conditions.

14. The mind-seal refers to a mental impression or intuitive certainty;
the mind is the Buddha-mind possessed by all, which can seal or assure
the Truth. Thus, the term indicates the intuitive method of the Ch'an
School, eschewing the spoken or written word. When Ch'an masters
confer the mind-seal on a student, they are, in effect, validating the
student's experience of enlightenment.

15. "Chewing and pecking" describes the pedagogical process that
transpires between Ch'an practitioners and their masters. The terms are
derived from the experience of a hatching chick. Chewing is the sucking
sound made by a chick inside its shell, indicating that it is ready to
hatch. In response to this action, the mother hen pecks at the shell from
the outside. Thus, the egg is cracked through the mutual efforts of the
chick and hen just as realization results from the mutual efforts of the
student and master. Chewing refers to the questions posed by the Ch'an
practitioner as a request for instruction from the master, while pecking
denotes the Ch'an master's teaching in response to this request that
facilitates the student's realization.

16. A well-known *kung-an* used by Ch'an masters. The Patriarch is
Bodhidharma, who came from India, which is west of China. He is
considered to be the first patriarch of the Ch'an School.

17. 'Emptiness' is the doctrine of sūnyatā which states that all
phenomena, including the ego, have no reality but are composed of a
certain number of elements.

18. Vulture Peak, situating near Rājaghrā, was the site of many
lectures given by the Buddha. The peak takes on the shape of the head
of a vulture, thus the peak is named Vulture Peak.

19. The *mani* pearl is a bright, luminous pearl symbolizing the Buddha and his doctrines. *Mani* can be translated as "as wished," hence the possessor of the pearl receives whatever he or she desires.

20. The four Celestial Kings were first introduced to China around the eighth century. They are considered to be the protectors of the four directions and live on the slopes of Mount Meru. They are also worshipped as guardians of the monasteries, and their images are usually placed at the entrance of most Chinese temples.

21. 'The Sound of One Hand Clapping' was a well known *kung-an* used by Ch'an practitioners as a subject for contemplation.

22. The rules of conduct expected of a Buddhist follower, which included abstention from intoxicants.

23. The Buddhist doctrine of the Twofold Truth, which is generally comprised of the conventional truth and the Ultimate Truth, suits knowledge to the level of the perceiver.

24. The stone path refers to the teaching of Ch'an Master Shih-t'ou whose name literally means "stone."

25. "The mind itself is Buddha" is the essential teaching introduced by Bodhidharma, the first Ch'an patriarch of China.

26. A self-cultivating fellow is one whose only concern is one's own cultivation and liberation.

27. Earth, water, fire, and air are the four elements of which all things are made.

28. The five aggregates are form, sensation, perception, mental formations, and consciousness. They are the components of an intelligent being, especially a human being.

29. This doctrine of emptiness is proclaimed in the *Heart Sutra*, a central text of Mahayana Buddhism.

30. At that time, Master Ma-tsu Tao-i was actively promoting Ch'an in Kiangsi, while Shih-t'ou was expounding its essence in Hunan. Ch'an practitioners sought the Dharma either with the former or the latter. Traveling back and forth between Kiangsi and Hunan became so popular that a Chinese expression referring to the practice is still used today.

31. In the phrase "to point a finger at the moon," the finger represents the sutras while the moon represents the doctrines. The finger can also represent the teacher who points out the enlightened experience (the moon) for a student.

32. The virtuous ones are those who have the potential to help one attain enlightenment.

33. The three virtues of nirvana are: (1) The virtue of the Buddha's eternal, spiritual body; (2) the virtue of the Buddha's wisdom, knowing all phenomena in their reality; and (3) the virtue of his freedom from all bonds.

34. The period of degeneration of the Buddha's teaching is the last of the three recognized periods, i.e. (1) the period of the correct doctrine of the Buddha, which was to last 500 to 1,000 years, followed by (2) the 1,000 year period of the semblance of correct doctrine, and (3) the period of decay and termination, lasting 10,000 years. Since the Buddha lived in the sixth century B.C.E., we are now in the third period.

35. A pagoda is an architectural form adapted from the Indian *stūpa*, erected on sites of special importance during the life of the Buddha or to house his relics. On his death, the relics of the Buddha are said to have been distributed to eight such sites. King Asoka, who reigned from 274 to 237 B.C.E., redistributed the Buddha's relics to 84,000 *stūpas*.

36. It is a common practice in the Ch'an tradition for those who have realized enlightenment to assume a "Dharma name" reflective of their new state of being, often bestowed by their masters.

37. In lieu of depending on scriptures, Ch'an Buddhism emphasizes "the transmission from mind to mind" in preserving its wisdom. A succession of patriarchs, or fully realized masters, originally provided

this line of transmission. Bodhidharma was known as the first patriarch in China (although in the line of Indian patriarchs he was the twenty-eighth), while Hui-nêng was the sixth and last patriarch in this lineage.

38. The "five desires" arise from the objects of the five senses—what we see, hear, smell, taste, or touch. This phrase also refers to wealth, sexuality, food and drink, fame, and sleep. The six dusts are produced by sense objects and the sense organs, namely sight, sound, smell, taste, touch, and consciousness. Since dust is dirt, these six dusts are the origin of all impurities.

39. The Chinese word translated as "worldly" (su^2) also means "tasteless," a possible pun on the discussion of all flavors.

40. Esoteric chanting based on magical formulas, mystic forms of prayer, or spells used by the Tantric order. They are often written in Sanskrit and have been found in China as early as the third century C.E.

41. A Ch'an board is a piece of wood 54 cm long, 6 cm wide, and 1 cm thick, with a hole near the top. A Ch'an master rests his back or hands on it when tired during meditation. A sutra stand is a low desk used when reading Buddhist scriptures.

42. "Wu" is similar to the English prefixes "un-" and "in-" which negate what follows them.

43. Rock refers to Ch'an Master Shih-t'ou Hsi-ch'ien. Shih-t'ou literally means rock in Chinese.

44. The monk in charge of managing the day to day administrative affairs of the monastery.

45. "Lung-man" literally means "Dragon Gate." It is a narrow pass along the Yellow River of China. The mountains on both sides of the river are so steep that they resemble a gate. "Lung-man" has been adopted by Ch'an practitioners to describe masters who are very strict with their students.

46. The five modes of existence include the various hells, hungry ghosts, animals, human beings, and divine beings. The six directions of reincarnation refer to the five modes of existence and the realm of the *asuras*. The ten Dharmaworlds include those of the hells, hungry ghosts, animals, *asuras*, humans, divine beings, *śravakas*, *pratyeka-buddhas*, *bodhisattvas*, and Buddhas.

47. "Karma-consciousness" implies that an unenlightened mind becomes disturbed due to ignorance.

48. The *Heart Sutra* has been translated several times under various titles. The generally accepted version is ascribed to the Indian monk Kumārajiva, who arrived in China in 401 C.E.

GLOSSARY

Arhan/arhat (Sanskrit)—the "worthy one," who has attained the highest level of "no-more-learning" on the religious path, and who possesses the certainty that all defilements and passions have been extinguished and will not arise again in the future. An arhan was an ideal goal of practice for practitioners of early Buddhism.

Avidyā (Sanskrit)—ignorance and the absence of enlightenment, darkness without illumination, ignorance that mistakes appearance for reality.

Bhūtatathatā (Sanskrit)—"suchness of existence"; the reality as opposed to the appearance of the phenomenal world. *Bhūtatathatā* is immutable and eternal, whereas forms and appearances arise, change, and pass away. This concept is used synonymously in Mahayana texts with the absolute or ultimate reality.

Bodhi (Sanskrit)—literally means "awakened." It is described as the awakening to one's own Buddha-nature or Buddha-essence, insight into the essential emptiness of the worlds.

Bodhidharma—the first patriarch of Ch'an Buddhism and the twenty-eighth patriarch of Indian Buddhism. He arrived in China from India around the sixth century C.E.; he was the Patriarch referred to in the famous *kung-an* "What Was the Meaning of the Patriarch's coming from the West."

Bodhicitta (Sanskrit)—the Buddha-mind; the mind of enlightenment.

Bodhisattva (Sanskrit)—literally an "enlightened being"; in general, it is a person seeking Buddhahood, but seeking it altruistically; whether monastic or layman, an individual seeks enlightenment to enlighten others, and he/she will sacrifice himself/herself to save others; he/she is devoid of egoism and devoted to helping others. All conscious beings having the Buddha-nature are natural bodhisattvas but require development.

Ch'an whisk (Chinese, *fu-tzu*)—an emblem of a Ch'an master's authority that figures prominently in the Ch'an method of teaching; it often was employed to communicate a point through gestures without relying on verbal language. It consists of a pointer with a brush or fly whisk attached to one end. In mundane life, it was used as a duster, and hence, symbolically, it is a tool for removing dust (ignorance) from a surface (the mirror of the original mind).

Conditioned co-production (Sanskrit, *pratītya-samutpāda*)—the core teaching of all Buddhist schools. It states that all mental and physical phenomena constituting individual existence are interdependent and mutually condition each other; at the same time, this describes what entangles sentient beings in samsāra.

Deva (Sanskrit)—celestial being or god, name of inhabitants of one of the good modes of existence who dwell in fortunate realms of the heavens but who, like all other beings, are subject to the cycle of rebirth. The gods lead a very long, happy life as a result of previous good deeds; however, this happiness is also the primary hindrance on their path to liberation. Because of this state of happiness, the devas cannot recognize the truth of suffering.

Dharma (Sanskrit)—the very core of Buddhist perception of reality and our role within that reality, used in various meanings of the cosmic law underlying our world; the teaching of the Buddha; moral behavior and ethical rules; reality of the general state of affairs; thing; phenomenon; mental content, object of thought, idea—a reflection of a thing in the human mind; term for the so-called factors of existence, which is considered as building blocks of the empirical personality and its world.

Dharmadhātu (Sanskrit)—literally means "realm of dharma"; a name for "things" in general, noumenal or phenomenal; for the physical universe, or any portion or phase of it; the unifying underlying spiritual reality regarded as the ground or cause of all phenomena.

Dharmakāya (Sanskrit)—"Dharma-body"; the embodiment of Truth and the Dharma, the "spiritual" or true body that represents the essence of Buddhahood; the universal standard of value.

Five dynasties (907-960 C.E.)—the later Liang, later T'ang, later Chin, later Han, and later Chou.

Kalpa (Sanskrit)—a period of time of incalculable duration. A *kalpa* also refers to a fabulous period of time and to the interval between the creation and total annihilation of a world or a universe.

Karma (Sanskrit)—literally means "deed" or "action"; universal law of cause and effect. According to the Buddhist view: An intentional deed produces an effect under certain circumstances; when it is ripe then it falls upon the one responsible.

Kuan-yin—the Chinese version of Avalokiteśvara; a bodhisattva known for her compassion, and often referred to as the Goddess of Compassion.

Kung-an (Japanese, *kōan*)—literally, "public document"; it originally meant a legal case constituting a precedent. In Ch'an, a kung-an is a phrase from a sutra or teaching on Ch'an realization, an episode from the life of an ancient master, each points to the nature of ultimate reality. Essential to a kung-an is paradox, i.e. that which is "beyond thinking," which transcends the logical or conceptual. Thus, since it cannot be solved by reason, a kung-an is not a riddle. Solving a kung-an requires a leap to another level of comprehension.

Lotus Sutra—the basic text of the T'ien-t'ai School, one of the eight schools of Chinese Buddhism. This text exerted a profound influence on the development of Buddhist doctrine in Tibet, China, and Japan.

Mahāprajñāpāramitā-sutra (Sanskrit)—also *Prajñāpāramitā-sutra*, literally meaning *"Great Sutra of the Wisdom that Reaches the Other Shore"*; term for a series of about forty Mahayana sutras, gathered together under this name because they all deal with the realization of *prajñā*. Probably, they were composed around the beginning of the Common Era. Some sutras are preserved in Sanskrit, however most of them are extant only in Chinese and Tibetan translation. The two most prominent *Prajñaparamita-sutras* in the West are the *Diamond Sutra* and the *Heart Sutra*.

Mahayana (Sanskrit)—"the great vehicle"; a major sect of Buddhism that teaches the doctrine of universal salvation through the efforts of bodhisattvas. It is the form of Buddhism prevalent in China, Korea, Japan, and Tibet; also known as Northern Buddhism as opposed to the Southern Buddhism of Sri Lanka, Thailand, and Burma.

Mañjuśrī—a bodhisattva known for his wisdom. He usually is depicted as holding the sword of wisdom and sitting on a lion, a symbol of stern majesty. In past incarnations he is identified as the parent of many Buddhas.

Nirvana (Sanskrit)—the goal of spiritual practice in all branches of Buddhism. In the understanding of early Buddhism, it is departure from the cycle of rebirths and entry into an entirely different mode of existence. It means freedom from the determining effect of karma and is a state that may be enjoyed in the present life.

No-mind (Chinese, *wu-hsin*; Japanese, *mu-shin*)—an expression for detachment of mind, a state of complete naturalness and freedom from dualistic thinking and feeling.

Prajñā (Sanskrit)—wisdom; a central notion of the Mahayana referring to an immediately experienced intuitive wisdom that cannot be conveyed by concepts or in intellectual terms. The realization of prajñā is often equated with the attainment of enlightenment and is one of the essential marks of Buddhahood.

Pure Land (Chinese, *ching-t'u*; Japanese, *jōdo*)—also known as Buddha-realms; according to the Mahayana Buddhism there are countless Buddhas, and countless pure lands also exist. According to folk belief, these pure lands are geographically localizable places of bliss; however, fundamentally they stand for aspects of the awakened state of mind.

Śākyamuni Buddha—"the sage of the Śākya tribe"; "*muni*" means a sage, holy person, or monk, that is, one who is benevolent, charitable, kind, and compassionate. He was the founder of Buddhism and was born in India over 2,500 years ago.

Samādhi (Sanskrit)—collectedness of the mind on a single object through gradual calming of mental activity. It is a non-dualistic state of consciousness in which the consciousness of the experiencing "subject" becomes one with the experienced "object."

Samantabhadra—the bodhisattva of universal goodness who is a symbol of the fundamental law. He usually is depicted riding a white six-tusked elephant.

Samsāra (Sanskrit)—literally means "journeying." The cycle of existences, a succession of rebirths that a being goes through within the various modes of existence until it has attained liberation and attained nirvana. The karma of the being is determinative of the type of rebirth that it will take.

Sangha (Sanskrit)—the Buddhist community; in a narrower sense the *Sangha* consists of monks, nuns, and novices who devote their lives to Buddhist practices toward the goal of achieving enlightenment by transcending *samsāra* and realizing nirvana. It represents a lifestyle in accordance with the pattern set by the Buddha, himself, as a middle way between the extremes of asceticism and sensuality. From a broader perspective, the *Sangha* also includes lay followers. The *Sangha* is one of the Three Precious Ones.

Śāstra (Sanskrit)—commentaries or treatises on Buddhist scriptures (sutras).

Six dynasties—the Wu dynasty (222-280 C.E.); the Eastern Chin dynasty (317-420 C.E.); the Sung dynasty (420-479 C.E.); the Ch'i dynasty (479-520 C.E.); the Liang dynasty (502-557 C.E.); and the Chen dynasty (557-589 C.E.); all of which had their capitals on the site of the modern city of Nanking.

Skandhas (Sanskrit)— the five aggregates, the components constituting an intelligent being, especially a human being. They are: (1) Form or matter, the physical manifestations that are the objects for the five sense organs; (2) Feeling or sensation, the functioning of the mind or senses in connection with events and things; (3) Conception, the discriminating functioning of the intellect; (4) Volition, the mental faculty concerned with judgments of liking and dislikes, good and evil, and so forth; and (5) Consciousness.

Sutra (Sanskrit)—"threads" or what is threaded together; the sacred scriptures of Buddhism.

Tathāgata (Sanskrit)—"thus gone" as well as "thus come," referring to the fact that the Buddha both comes by and goes to the Path of enlightenment; one of the ten titles of the Buddha used by his followers, and also used by the Buddha as a form of self-reference.

Tathāgatagarbha (Sanskrit)—the womb or matrix of *Tathāgata*. It is the source of all phenomena: all created things are in the *Tathāgatagarbha*, which is the womb that gives birth to them all. The *Tathāgatagarbha* is also the storehouse of the Buddha's teaching.

Ten directions—the eight points of the compass in addition to the nadir and the zenith.

Three Precious Ones (Sanskrit, *Triratna*)—the three essential components of Buddhism: the Buddha, the Dharma, and the *Sangha*; i.e. the Awakened One, the Truth expounded by him, and the followers living in accordance with this Truth. The Three Precious Ones are objects of veneration. Buddhists take refuge in them by pronouncing the threefold refuge formula, thus acknowledging themselves publicly to be Buddhists.

Three worlds (Sanskrit, Triloka)—(1) the realm of sensuous desire inclusive of sexuality and food, encompassing the six heavens of desire, the human world, and the various hells; (2) the realm of form or what is substantial and resistant; situated above the lust-world, it contains bodies, places, and phenomena that are mystically wondrous—a semi-material conception; here desire for sexuality and food falls away, but the capacity for enjoyment continues. It has eighteen heavens; (3) the formless realm of pure spirit lacking bodies, places, or things to which human terms apply; here the mind dwells in mystic contemplation.

Ti-tsang—a bodhisattva recognized as the guardian of the Earth. Though associated with the dead and the various hells, his role is that of savior, in accordance with his vow to postpone his own attainment of nirvana until the hells have been emptied.

Tonsure—to become tonsured means to have one's head shaved, a ritual signifying ordination or acceptance into the Buddhist monastic order enacted for both monks and nuns.

Ts'an ch'an monk—the Chinese term *"ts'an ch'an"* means "to reflect on," "counsel," "visit a superior," as well as "an assembly or a gathering for the purpose of meditation, preaching, or worship"; hence, this term describes a serious practitioner of Ch'an.

Vimalakīrti (Sanskrit)—Vimalakīrti is the principal character of the *Vimalakīrti Sutra*. He is a wealthy and highly cultivated lay Buddhist practitioner who lives in the midst of worldly life while treading on the Path of the bodhisattvas.

Yāna (Sanskrit)—a vehicle; a term applied to Buddhism as a means by which a practitioner travels on the Path to enlightenment. The different vehicles correspond to views of the spiritual "journey" that differ as to the basic attitude of the practitioner and the means of making progress on the way. There are categories of one, two, three, four, and five. The most common divisions are two yānas and three yānas.

Yogācāra (Sanskrit)—a Buddhist school of the Mahayana tradition founded by Asanga during the fourth century C.E. The central notion of *Yogācāra* is that things exist only as processes of knowing, not as "objects"; anything outside the knowing processes has no reality.

ABOUT THE AUTHOR

Venerable Master Hsing Yun was born in China in 1926. He became a monk at the age of twelve and was fully ordained by 1941. Eight years later, he arrived in Taiwan, where he undertook a revitalization of Buddhism, the success of which is mirrored in the numerous temples, publications, social, educational, and cultural projects that have proliferated under his guidance. Through the International Buddhist Progress Society, centers for the propagation of Buddhism as well as the Chinese culture have been established throughout the world. Master Hsing Yun has been recognized for his bold and innovative methods of propagating the Dharma to meet contemporary human needs.

Master Hsing Yun has contributed numerous publications in the field of Buddhism. In addition to the ten volumes of *Master Hsing Yun's Account of Ch'an* in Chinese, he has served as Editor-in-Chief for an eight-volume *Fo Kuang Dictionary of Buddhism* (1988) and a sixteen volume *Āgama* (1984). His other works include *Śākyamuni Buddha* (1955), *Buddha's Ten Great Disciples* (1959), and *The Sutra of the Eight Great Enlightenments* (1960). In addition, several volumes of his collected lectures on Buddhism have been published in both Chinese and English.

The Master's academic achievements are numerous. Currently, he is the President of Hsi Lai University in Los Angeles. Furthermore, he has chaired organizing committees for international conferences which include the International Buddhist Conference, the International Conference on Ch'an Buddhism, and the World Fellowship of Buddhists.

In 1988, Master Hsing Yun led a Buddhist delegation to the People's Republic of China which was the first such delegation that visited Mainland China since the Cultural Revolution. While visiting important Buddhist sites, he and his group met with top Chinese officials to discuss the future of Buddhism in China.

ASIAN THOUGHT AND CULTURE is designed to cover three inter-related projects: (1) *Asian Classics Translation* (including those modern Asian works that have been generally accepted as "classics"), with notes and commentaries provided; (2) *Asian and Comparative Philosophy and Religion,* including excellent and publishable Ph.D. dissertations, scholarly monographs, or collected essays; and (3) *Asian Thought and Culture in a Broader Perspective,* covering exciting and publishable works in Asian culture, history, political and social thought, education, literature, music, fine arts, performing arts, martial arts, medicine, etc.

The series editor is:

Charles Wei-hsun Fu
Department of Religion
Temple University
Philadelphia, PA 19122

DATE DUE

AUG 2 5 2004			

HIGHSMITH 45-220